UNITED STATES

AN ILLUSTRATED HISTORY

CONTENTS

~

Introduction 6

An Age of Rediscovery 8
1400-1749
The First Americans 10 • *The Vikings* 12 • *The First Arrivals* 16
The First Settlers 18 • *The Missionaries* 20 • *The Dispersal of Slaves* 24

New People in a New World 28
1750-1799
The First Colonies 30 • *The Revolutionary War* 34
Declaration of Independence 38 • *Development of the Political Parties* 40 • *The Cotton Gin* 42

Forming a More Perfect Union 44
1800-1849
The Louisiana Purchase 46 • *Lewis and Clark* 48 • *Trade on the Water* 52
The Industrial Revolution 54 • *Westward Expansion* 56 • *The Trail of Tears* 60 • *Texas Revolution* 62
Remembering the Alamo 64 • *Parceling Out the Land* 68 • *Manifest Destiny* 70 • *The Rush for Gold* 72

A Nation Comes of Age 74
1850-1899
The Underground Railroad 76 • *The Pony Express* 78 • *The Civil War* 80
Emancipation Proclamation 84 • *Reconstruction* 86
The Railroads 88 • *American West* 92 • *Forging the Future* 96 • *Organizing the Workers* 98
National Parks 100 • *The Telegraph and Telephone* 104

A Nation at War 106
1900-1949
Pioneers of Aviation 108 • *Social Reform* 112 • *The Automobile* 114
World War One 118 • *Women Go to the Polls* 122 • *Going Dry* 124 • *Pictures That Talk* 126
Waves of New Americans 130 • *Riding the Airwaves* 134 • *The Stock Market Crash* 136
The New Deal 138 • *On the Reservation* 140
World War Two 144 • *The Manhattan Project* 148

Decades of Change 150
1950-PRESENT
Small Screens 152 • *Stemming the Communist Tide* 154 • *Fight for Civil Rights* 156
Tragedy and Loss 160 • *The War in Southeast Asia* 162 • *The First Small Steps* 166
Misbehaving in America 170 • *The New Global Tensions* 172
The Gulf War 174 • *The Internet Takes Off* 178 • *Attacks on America* 180
A Second War in the Gulf 182 • *Americans Explore* 186

INDEX AND ILLUSTRATIONS CREDITS 188

PREVIOUS PAGES: *Taken in 1937 by renowned photographer Dorothea Lange,*
two men on their way to Los Angeles, California, walk down a dirt road past a billboard
advertisement for a more expensive way to travel: the train.
OPPOSITE: *In 1909, American painter Frederic Remington created this work,*
The Outlier, *of a lone Native American astride his horse.*
Today, the painting can be seen in the Brooklyn Museum.

INTRODUCTION

John Carlin, Head Archivist of the United States

The National Archives and Records Administration is our nation's record keeper, and as Archivist of the United States, I have the great honor to oversee a collection of the documents, photographs, video and audiotapes, and other records that have been witness to American history as it was made. These billions of records tell the first-hand stories of both our triumphs and tragedies as a nation and illustrate the passion, genius, and spirit that have shaped America since its beginning.

At the National Archives we work to preserve and provide access to the records of the federal government for the American people. For without these records, we would not know or be able to understand our past. We would not be able to hold our elected officials accountable for their actions. We would not be able to claim our rights and entitlements. Without these records, we would no longer live in a democracy.

Among the most famous records we care for are the Declaration of Independence, the Constitution, and the Bill of Rights—collectively known as the Charters of Freedom. Other documents, such as Eli Whitney's patent for the cotton gin, the Homestead Act, the Emancipation Proclamation, and the Civil Rights Act of 1964, to name a few, have helped mold our national character and reflect our changing culture. Still other records such as the papers of Presidential administrations, World War II battle plans, or routine files from the State Department capture glimpses of history in the making and chronicle the actions of our government.

However, our history is found not only in constitutional amendments, Presidential proclamations, and well-known historical documents. It is found also in the veteran's records of the brave men and women who have fought for our country; in the immigration records of the people whose dreams have shaped our country; and the census records that enumerate each individual, family, and community that made up our country at a given point in time.

Each record that we hold tells a story. Some of these stories changed history, while some quietly resonated in the lives of individuals. But each story is significant as they all weave together to form the ever-growing tapestry that is our national history. To remember the stories and details of our history is honorable work.

The pages of this book represent more than 500 years of the history of our nation. Each page unfolds a new event, a new piece of the masterwork that is the United States as we know it today. As a collection it captures all of our country's pivotal moments of decision. It shows a nation at war, unfortunately several times including once with itself; a nation struggling to have its existence recognized; and after this hard-won recognition, a nation struggling with growing pains as it inches across the continent. In its later pages, this book bears evidence of a maturing nation measuring its place in a world order. Having satisfactorily set itself a course, it begins to test how this course will be received.

There is no doubt that we can see the journey of the United States illustrated as Americans declare their independence, rally for their rights, walk on the moon, and face crises at home and abroad. But we also find America in the joy and everyday activities that make up people's lives. Through the early beginnings of movies, the sounds of radio performers, the dramas and comedies appearing on the small screen, up through the amazing innovations of the Internet: Americans have embraced new technologies to feed and entertain their minds.

In the history of America, there are George Washington and Abraham Lincoln, Eli Whitney and Alexander Graham Bell, Susan B. Anthony and Martin Luther King, Amelia Earhart and Neil Armstrong—these are the Americans familiar. They are pioneers of politics, inventions, civil rights, and exploration. But there are even more American pioneers whose names remain unknown and unfamiliar—the colonists, homesteaders, immigrants, farmers, shopkeepers, riveters, and veterans who pieced together the seams of the story of the United States.

Like the records held in the National Archives, this book tells the collective history of the people of the United States. Each chapter of history builds upon those before it, as each generation of Americans learns from the sacrifices, successes, and lessons of those that came before. Each chapter features images that illustrate watershed events, important places, key figures, and even period documents and items from different eras. This text brings to life the events that solidify history and perpetuate its telling.

Every day we make history, as our government does the work of a powerful democracy, our scientists bring us bigger and better advances, and we each live our individual lives. Each day brings changes that will shape the path of the United States for generations to come. And in the future, the days we live now will be as rich in history as the book you now hold in your hands.

BELOW: *Teddy Roosevelt, later the 26th President of the U.S., stands proudly with his troops atop San Juan Hill in Cuba. Their successful charge captured a blockhouse and opened the route to Santiago, assuring American victory in the Spanish-American War.*

1400
THROUGH
1749

AN AGE *of* REDISCOVERY

"T he United States themselves are essentially the greatest poem," wrote Walt Whitman. Its stanzas are expressed in its climate, its people, and its land. The lands of North America are enormously varied. The shorelines of the East Coast rise to meet the Appalachian highlands. The central lowlands give way to the Great Plains. The Rocky Mountains and the Colorado Plateau, home to grand canyons and towering buttes and mesas, melt into basins and ranges and the Columbia Plateau. The Sierra Nevada and the Cascades edge the western ocean.

From 1400–1749, the population of North America changed drastically. The lands were originally peopled by Native Americans. Their densest populations lived on the coast of California, around Lake Michigan, and along the Eastern seaboard and in central Florida.

Europeans first made contact when Leif Eriksson and the Vikings established a North American colony around A.D. 1000. The Europeans would not gain a strong foothold in the "New World" until after Christopher Columbus's expedition in 1492.

After Europeans came to North America, they caused major conflicts with and shifts in Native American populations. Spanish missionaries, French traders, and English farmers transformed North America and its lands. African slaves first arrived in 1619. Long before this, however, it was clear that these new arrivals would transform this continent and create a governing system based on European accession of American lands.

Created in 1607, this detail from a map of the world shows the Western Hemisphere surrounded by a wealth of allegorical figures.

The FIRST AMERICANS

Early Native Civilizations

The very first Americans were the paleo-Indians—or the "ancestral" Indians. Several million strong, they populated nearly every corner of the continent, developing societies based on hunting and gathering, farming, fishing, and nomadic roaming after herds of game.

With much of the oceans' waters tied up in glaciers, a thousand-mile-wide land bridge linked Siberia with the Alaskan tip of North America. Over the centuries, migrants—who had no notion that they were crossing a bridge—flowed across the North American continent. Some went to the south to reach, by 9000 B.C., the southernmost tip of South America; others moved eastward across the top of North America.

The Inuit were part of this gradual migration of peoples into North America from Siberia between 10,000 and 40,000 years ago. As they arrived, they slowly moved eastward, reaching

---

THE HAWAIIAN ISLANDS

When Capt. James Cook made landfall on the islands of Hawaii in 1778 the population was perhaps 300,000, descendants of those who had sailed from the Marquises Islands some 1,500 years before. Food was plentiful, the climate was sublime—but they were ruled by a religion that included many taboos. For instance, it was forbidden for men and women to eat together or for the shadow of a commoner to fall on a chief.

After gaining control of Hawaii, King Kamehameha in 1790 launched a conquest of islands to the west. Within 20 years all were under his rule. "Endless is the good that I have given you to enjoy," he told his people from his deathbed in 1819. Within six months his successors had overturned traditions and abolished most of the extreme taboos. ■

Greenland. They developed the Thule culture—harpoons, stone lamps, fishhooks, bows and arrows. Those moving across northern Alaska and Canada were probably pursuing bowhead whales, as they migrated. Southern migrants moved across broad grasslands, preying on mammoths, caribou, and giant bison.

Archaeologists trace the routes of these paleo-Indians through their artifacts—especially their projectile points. Chipped Clovis points tipped spears throughout the continent by 9200 B.C.; later Folsom points had long flutes along their faces; by 2500 B.C. some Eskimos were using abrasives such as sand in water to grind points from slate; between 3000 and 1200 B.C. hammered copper points appeared.

The paleo-Indians' world began to change 10,000 years ago, after the earth warmed and the ice began to retreat. Deserts and plains took over much of the West, grasslands spread across the prairies, and forests blanketed the East. The farming revolution—knowledge of planting and harvesting, especially of three important crops: squash, corn, and beans—began in the Southwest and spread eastward, freeing people to develop a more settled existence, which in turn led to the eventual emergence of the continent's great early civilizations.

One of the first of the true Native American civilizations was the Hohokam, an agricultural community that emerged along the Gila and Salt Rivers in the Southwest deserts about 300 B.C. Among their achievements were America's first known irrigation canal and some of North America's first pottery. They lived in pit houses near their fields and raised two crops a year. Through contact with natives in Mexico they learned to build oval ball courts for their games.

Perhaps the most impressive civilization was

that of the Anasazi, who came later. They built multifamily pueblos. They devised elaborate irrigation systems and studied the stars from observatories. They never learned to use the wheel, nor did they have beasts of burden, yet they constructed hundreds of miles of roads across the sun-blasted Southwest.

In present-day New Mexico the Anasazi built their most impressive city—Pueblo Bonito, in Chaco Canyon. The resources required for building such a city were tremendous: roughly 200,000 timbers, some weighing 600 pounds and transported from pine forests 40 miles away. An average room in Pueblo Bonito took about 100,000 pounds of stone, 33,000 pounds of clay, and 1,000 gallons of water.

In the East, people settled into villages by A.D. 500. Two waves of culture rolled across the East: the Aden way of life, which flourished from about 500 to 1 B.C., and the more complex Hopewell culture, which peaked between A.D. 1 and 300. Both cultures crossed linguistic and geographic barriers; through trade, communities learned about each other's crops and culture.

Named for the Indian farms found along the Mississippi River, the Mississippian people were accomplished artisans. A hallmark of the Mississippian culture was reliance, for the first time in the East, on farming as the main food source. Corn, beans, and squash were staples. Most impressive was their trade network, which spread all over North America and included the nomadic tribes on the Great Plains, the woodland Indians of the Northeast, and other Mississippian tribes up and down the river. The largest settlement, Cahokia, sat near the confluence of the Mississippi, Missouri, and Illinois Rivers. At its apex, the city was home to 10,000 residents, but on festival days the population probably grew to 40,000—a population greater than London's at that time.

Mississippian peoples were keenly territorial. They wrested land from one another and dispatched warriors to carry on tribal feuds. By the time Europeans found the Mississippian centers, they were fatally weakened by drought and intertribal warfare.

ABOVE: *Cliff Palace, largest of the Anasazi pueblos, clings to a shelf in Mesa Verde National Park. Built between A.D. 1190 and 1280, it housed perhaps a hundred "ancient ones."*

The VIKINGS

~

New Founders Reach the Shores

Around the year 1000, a group of about 30 Vikings led by Leif Eriksson landed in the upper right-hand corner of North America, near what would one day be Newfoundland. The Vikings were the first new arrivals to this land, which had been populated for over 7,000 years.

The Vikings hailed from Scandinavia. Between the 8th and the 11th centuries, they colonized large sections of Europe. Their very name—*vikingr* in Old Norse—meant far-traveler. They may have been urged seaward by overpopulation at home, where they worked largely as farmers. Their colonies arose over much of the known world: from England and Ireland to the Seine; from the Orkneys, the Faroes, the Shetlands, and the Hebrides to the Iberian Peninsula; even eastward from the Baltic into Russia. In the ninth century they made landfall on Iceland and in the tenth Greenland. Erik the Red named the frigid island Greenland in an early public relations campaign so that "men would be drawn to go there."

Near their Newfoundland site one of their number found wild grapes growing in the forest, so they called the newly discovered land Vinland. Accounts report, "Nature was so generous here that . . . no cattle would need any winter fodder, but could graze outdoors." The climate was mild—grass stayed green even in winter—and salmon were plentiful in the streams. Leif and his men hauled lumber home to Greenland—it was valuable in the nearly treeless country—and grapes, probably as raisins or wine. They talked enthusiastically of the new landfall, prompting more expeditions. Thorfinn Thorsdarsson Karlsefni led one that consisted of perhaps 135 men and 15 women, along with livestock in at least three ships. They used Leif's camp as a base and lived there for several years, shipping cargoes of lumber, pelts, and other local goods home. One of the expeditions settled for a time at the head of Newfoundland's Great Northern Peninsula, at a place now called L'Anse aux Meadows.

The question of Viking settlements in the New World was long debated by scholars—some doubting their existence, others persuaded by the Norse sagas that they had existed. In 1960 Norwegian writer and archaeologist Helge Ingstad came to L'Anse aux Meadows searching for Norse landing places. A local showed him a group of overgrown hillocks and ridges that turned out to be structural remains. Ingstad and his wife, archaeologist Anne Stine Ingstad, directed a dig at the site.

From underneath the hills emerged Viking houses, workshops, and even a blacksmith shop. Here iron had been smelted for the first time in the New World. Remains from the blacksmith shop included iron boat nails. A knitting needle proved that women had been among the colony. And one small find seemed to prove conclusively that these had been Vikings: a bronze, ring-headed pin used to fasten their cloaks.

In the mid-1970s archaeologists with Parks Canada, the Canadian Park Service, continued digging at L'Anse aux Meadows, primarily in a peat bog. Diggers found some 2,000 pieces of worked wood, much of it shavings and scraps from work Norsemen had done on trees before shipping timber home. After the dig was completed and documented, Parks Canada, to protect the site for future study, buried the entire area under a layer of white sand and covered it again with fresh turf. L'Anse aux Meadows is the only confirmed Viking site in North America.

RIGHT: *Fearsome Viking raiders prepare to invade France in an illustration from a ninth-century manuscript.*
NEXT: *Along these shores of Gros Morne National Park in Canada, Viking settlers may have landed in the year 1000.*

The FIRST ARRIVALS

Europeans and the New World

Amerigo Vespucci lost the race but won the banner: History books dub Christopher Columbus the "Discoverer of America," but Amerigo's name became attached to the continent. He voyaged to the New World—another name he bequeathed—at least twice and maybe as many as four times. An accomplished merchant and explorer, he was for a while the influential "master navigator" of Seville. His duties included fitting out ships, including the vessels used by Columbus in later trips. The two probably met when Columbus returned from his first voyage.

Vespucci's expeditions to the New World occurred between 1497 and 1504. One kept him at sea from May 1499 to June 1500 and took him to the coast of Guyana. From there he headed south and became the first European to reach the mouth of the Amazon River. In May 1501 he set off on another voyage, which took him to the coast of Brazil; he may have gone as far south as Patagonia. At first, Vespucci believed he was close to Asia, but the more trips he made the less certain he became that he had reached the Orient. Finally he became convinced that he was sailing in previously unknown territories. Within a few years a German cartographer suggested that these new lands should be named in his honor: "from Amerigo the discoverer . . . as if it were the land of Americus or America." At first his name was attached only to South America, but it came to include both continents of the New World.

Amerigo's famous colleague Christopher Columbus made four journeys across the Atlantic, in the service of Spain, between the years of 1492 and 1504. His discoveries set off a European era of exploration, exploitation, and colonization of the Americas.

Columbus's original goal was to find a westerly route to the Orient but, like his peers, he expected the Orient to be significantly closer to Europe. When he made landfall at Cuba, Haiti, and San Salvador, he thought the islands were off the coast of China and Japan. He called the native peoples he met Indians, a misnomer that has lasted for more than 500 years.

To Europeans, his discoveries were a triumph, bringing profit and opening vast new territories to expansion and settlement; to the peoples who were indigenous to the New World, his landfall was a tragedy. For them there followed centuries of exploitation, slavery, and death from diseases against which they had no resistance.

Vespucci and Columbus were not the only early explorers to cross the broad oceans. In 1497 Venetian John Cabot reached the coast of Newfoundland, and a year later Vasco da Gama sailed to India via the Cape of Good Hope. In 1500 Portuguese explorer Gaspar Côrte-Real spotted Greenland and explored the coast of Newfoundland. His sailors reported "men of the forest and white bears." That same year Pedro Alvares Cabral claimed Brazil for Portugal. In 1513 Vasco Núñez de Balboa sighted the Pacific Ocean after crossing the Isthmus of Panama from the Caribbean. In 1508 Juan Ponce de León explored and colonized Puerto Rico. Nine years later Francisco Fernández de Córdoba discovered the Yucatán Peninsula and battled the Maya, and just two years after that Magellan set out to achieve Columbus's goal—to reach the Orient by sailing west. He was killed in the Philippines, but one of his five ships made the first world circumnavigation in 1522.

Many were motivated to come to the New World in hopes of finding the silks and spices of the Orient that would make them fortunes at home. Later, others hoped to find a water route through or around America that would take them to Asia.

The Spanish often claimed to be exploring in order to find more souls for God, but they had economic motives too. Bernal Díaz wrote that they came "to serve God . . . to give light to those in darkness and also to get rich." Tales of fabulous mines and jeweled cities lured them. A few found the wealth they were looking for: Cortés in Mexico and Pizarro in Peru amassed great riches.

Those who found no gold found slave labor instead. *Encomiendas*, feudal-like land grants, gave some Spaniards vast land holdings. While missionaries converted the Indians, working to save their souls, most Spaniards enslaved them. Assaulted by their masters and by the diseases the Europeans had brought with them, millions of Indians died. Much of their art and architecture also was destroyed as Spanish culture was spread across the New World.

Spain, France, England, and Holland planted their flags on huge territories in the Americas. They laid claim first to coastal lands or sites on the big rivers—the Rio Grande, Hudson, Mississippi—where trading ships could navigate. As nations of Europe competed for New World colonies, geographic knowledge of the discoveries spread quickly. Cartography kept pace, and maps began to reflect actual coastlines and islands.

OPPOSITE: *This 16th-century print portrays Portuguese explorer Vasco da Gama, discoverer of the sea route from Europe to India.*

BELOW: *American illustrator N.C. Wyeth painted in 1927* Ships of Christopher Columbus at Sea, *one of his many illustrations of tales of adventure and exploration.*

The FIRST SETTLERS

European Claims and Exploration

Between 1492, when Columbus first made landfall, and the early 1600s, a long and distinguished list of explorers crossed the ocean: They included Cabot, Balboa, Ponce de León, Cortes, Verrazano, Cartier, de Soto, Coronado, Champlain, and Hudson, among others. As soon as the explorers' reports were received at home in Europe, the great powers began claiming chunks of the New World for themselves.

The European powers—the Spanish, French, English, and Dutch, especially—tried to establish permanent settlements in America. French and English privateers wanted coastal bases, and their governments wanted Spain's treasure pipeline siphoned. In 1598 the Spaniards forged up the Rio Grande to San Gabriel, where they founded a settlement. In the north, French sea captain Samuel de Champlain established the first French colony in Canada at Quebec.

Sir Walter Raleigh, Queen Elizabeth I's favorite explorer and privateer, put together the first expeditions to the New World. Elizabeth was hopeful for the same things other European monarchs wanted: a passage to Asia, the fabled gold mines of the Americas, and another way to challenge Spain. She chartered Raleigh to explore the eastern coast of North America and the "remote, heathen and barbarous lands" inland.

Such charters gave explorers wide leeway: they could claim lands in the name of their sovereign; they could organize settlers and ship them across the ocean; they could establish and rule the settlements. The charters of England gave colonists the same rights and privileges of Englishmen at home: to own property, to be tried by juries of their peers, and to be ruled by a representative government.

Off North Carolina in 1585, in Roanoke Island's Pamlico Sound, two of Raleigh's captains found seashores that were "sandy and low toward the water's side, but so full of grapes that the very beating and surge of the sea overflowed the fruit." They also found Indians farming, fishing, and hunting and thought them "most gentle, loving and faithful, void of all guile and treason."

Raleigh, remembering his Virgin Queen, called the place Virginia, and the first English child to be born in the New World, Virginia Dare, was also named for the Queen. But the settlement on Roanoke Island was in trouble from the beginning. There was no anchorage deep enough to service privateers. The colonists, busy looking for gold, neglected to plant crops, so Roanoke failed as a commercial colony, too. By

CAPTAIN JOHN SMITH

Captain John Smith and a team of 14 English colonists made a remarkable journey in June 1608. Setting out on the second day of the month, the team embarked from the Virginia colony to navigate and document the waters of the Chesapeake Bay and the lands surrounding it. Traveling in a 30-foot boat, the team covered more than 1,700 miles. Their expedition would last for three months as they explored the intricate waterways.

Smith kept careful records, and sketches of his journey served as the foundation for a detailed Chesapeake map, drafted in 1612, that served as the definitive map of the region for over a century. Smith's observations continue to be a valuable resource today because they reveal the rich ecosystem of the 17th-century Chesapeake: Smith describes an "abundance of fish, lying so thick with their heads above the water . . . neither better fish, more plenty . . . had any of us ever seen in any place so swimming in the water." He also documented the many successful Native American cultures who lived alongside the Bay. ∎

1590, all evidence of the colony and its colonists had vanished.

The next English attempt at a colony in the New World happened 17 years later when the Virginia Company, a joint stock corporation, was chartered by King James I. They raised money and their first three ships carried 108 settlers. They came ashore on the James River and founded Jamestown. The Virginia Company advertised for more settlers, promising paradise, where the oranges, apples, lemons were "so delicious that whoever tastes them will despise the insipid watery taste of those we have in England." But the swamps bred malarial mosquitoes, and contaminated water caused dysentery. Indians were a constant menace. By 1609 most settlers had died.

It was tobacco that saved the day. Indians had long been growing the crop, but Londoners found the American strain too harsh. Farmer John Rolfe found a milder variety that pleased, and it swept across Europe. Soon successful tobacco farms lined the James, and between 1619 and 1624, 5,000 English settlers came to Virginia.

In the meantime, Henry Hudson, another explorer seeking the elusive northwest passage, had found his way 150 miles up the river that would one day bear his name. It was beautiful country, where Indians were clothed in the skins of fur-bearing animals—beaver, otter, mink, bear. Henry's employer, the Dutch East India Company, launched successful settlements in the Hudson Valley to export furs. They built forts on the tip of Manhattan Island and near present-day Albany to service the fur trade. From the forts, European settlers moved steadily inland.

On December 21, 1620, English settlers came ashore at Plymouth, on Cape Cod. They fancied themselves a stronger breed than the English who had preceded them. One wrote, "It is not with us as with other men, whom small things can discourage."

ABOVE: *A modern-day reenactor scales the rigging of this reconstructed 17th-century ship at Jamestown, Virginia, the first successful English colony in North America.*

The MISSIONARIES

Settling the Land, Spreading the Word

Christian soldiers spreading The Word, missionaries found fertile ground in the populations of the New World, while emigrants fleeing organized religions in Europe found a place to worship free of interference.

Spain, having agreed by treaty with Portugal to divide the non-Christian world into exclusive spheres of influence, won the right to the New World. Few Spanish explorers embarked without representatives of the church aboard their ships. They were not always welcomed warmly by the Native Americas there: In 1549, angered by visits of Spanish slavers, Florida Indians killed Dominican Luis Cancer de Bastro when he landed at what is now called Tampa Bay in one of Spain's first purely missionary expeditions.

Vast areas of the West and Southwest claimed by Spain were largely empty of Spaniards. A thin line of military presidios and missions held their territory. In 1718 a Franciscan mission was built in the Spanish outpost of San Antonio de Valero, and by 1770 Franciscan missionaries had introduced draft animals and European farming methods to Indians living near Monterey and San Diego. To combat damage done to crops by seasonal flooding and drought, the friars experimented successfully with dams and aqueducts.

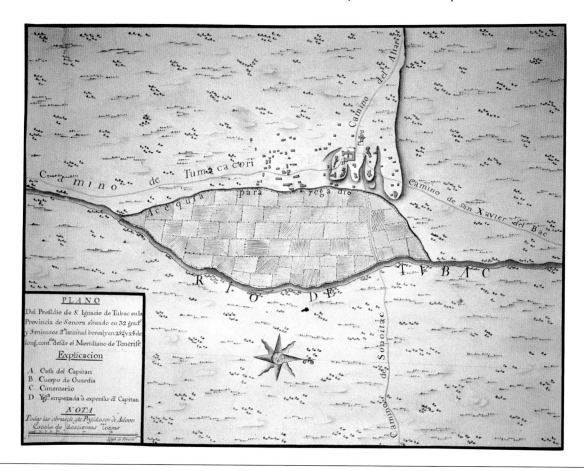

Franciscan Fathers built 21 missions in California, beginning in 1769 with the founding of Misíon San Diego de Alcala. Their most renowned mission was San Juan Capistrano, built between Los Angeles and San Diego. It is still famous for the legendary return each year in March of its resident swallows.

To solidify Spanish control—and also to prevent other powers from staking claims in the territory—the Fathers built their missions about a day's ride apart. But their primary motivation was to encourage literacy among the Indians and to convert them to Christianity. Spanish settlements grew up around the missions, each with a military garrison, or presidio, which served to protect the missions and the colonists. The friars introduced the first domestic grapes and oranges to the lands, agricultural imports that would one day benefit the economy of the state of California.

But the effect on the Indians was not benign. The Spaniards felt themselves to be superior to their charges and did not hesitate to treat the Indians as less than human. And as elsewhere in the world, the missionaries, in their zeal, destroyed the pillars of the Indians' society, which collapsed under missionary rule.

On the eastern side of North America, other faiths were taking root among the colonists who settled there. New strains of religious thought grew out of controversy in the Massachusetts Bay Colony. Roger Williams was banished in 1635 for challenging the church. A champion of Native Americans' rights, Williams reminded the Puritan elders that "forced worship stinks in God's nostrils."

Another dissident, Anne Hutchinson, held weekly meetings to discuss sermons and theology. At first, her gatherings were attended solely by women, but as interest grew in their discussions, men joined the group. Hutchinson and her followers held views that differed from those of the Puritans'. Because of her ideas, Hutchinson would be tried, excommunicated, and banished from the Massachusetts Bay Colony. In 1638, she and her followers moved to Rhode Island, settling near what is now Portsmouth. Rhode Island, which detractors called "Rogue's Island," became a refuge for Quakers, Jews, Baptists, and other religious dissidents.

The Puritans' hold on religion would not last, and religious diversity did eventually come to New England. In 1701 William III chartered a society to support Anglican missionary efforts in the colonies, and in 1709 a Quaker meetinghouse was built in Boston, Massachusetts. Congregations generally shared Martin Luther's vision of Christianity: The Bible—not church tradition— was the sole authority and gave believers immediate access to God. Between the 1720s and 1740s, the Eastern colonies experienced a series of religious revivals called the Great Awakening. Ministers, like Jonathan Edwards and George Whitefield, delivered powerful sermons emphasizing the individual's relationship with the Divine. Institutions of learning arose to train new ministers; two such colleges later grew into Princeton and Brown University.

By 1750 a religious impulse, largely Protestant and reform-minded, had taken root in Britain's New World settlements. Churches "of the Congregational Way" dominated New England. Baptist dissenters moved to Rhode Island and then spread south. Pennsylvania was home to Quakers, Moravians, and Mennonites.

Pluralism was also the rule in southern colonies, though the number of parishes lagged behind "well-churched" New England. Anglicans were in the majority in southern areas, even in Maryland, which had begun as a Roman Catholic colony. By 1750 these and many other religions made a diversity of devotions uniquely tolerated in the New World. In 1791 the colonists, having won independence, enshrined Williams's doctrine in the Bill of Rights, making freedom of conscience a matter of law.

OPPOSITE: *Structures of the Spanish presidio cluster around a crossroads near the Tubac River in present-day Arizona.*
NEXT: *This view of the Mission San Juan Capistrano in California shows the Bell Wall, one of the oldest standing segments of the mission, which was founded in 1776.*

The DISPERSAL of SLAVES

The Spread of Human Bondage

bout the last of August came in a dutch man of warre that sold us twenty Negers," wrote John Rolfe of Jamestown, Virginia, in his record of 1619. These were the first blacks known to have entered a mainland English colony. They probably were actually indentured servants, in which case they would have been freed after a fixed period of service.

The term "Negro slave" first appeared in legislation in Virginia in 1659, and in 1662 it was decreed that the child of a black woman "shall be bond or free according to the condition of the mother," which effectively made slavery hereditary. A 1705 Virginia law broadened and codified the rights of white servants, but it also defined the

THE MIDDLE PASSAGE

laudah Equiano's 1789 autobiography is one of the strongest testaments against slavery. Born ca 1745 in what is now Nigeria, he was kidnapped as a child and sold into slavery in the New World. Equiano purchased his freedom in his early 20s; he moved to London and became involved in the abolitionist movement. In 1789 he wrote *The Interesting Narrative of the Life of Olaudah Equiano, or Gustavus Vassa the African*, which documented the brutality of slavery. His description of the Middle Passage, the journey from Africa to the New World, reveals the conditions Africans endured aboard slave traders' ships: "The stench of the hold . . . was so intolerably loathsome, that it was dangerous to remain there for any time . . . The closeness of the place, and the heat of the climate, added to the number in the ship, which was so crowded that each had scarcely room to turn himself, almost suffocated us. This . . . brought on a sickness among the slaves, of which many died, thus falling victims to the improvident avarice . . . of their purchasers . . . The shrieks of the women, and the groans of the dying, rendered the whole a scene of horror almost inconceivable." ■

role of black slaves as "real estate [which] shall descend unto heirs and widows." If slaves escaped, anyone might legally "kill and destroy" them.

Colonists soon found that slaves were cheaper labor than indentured servants. Between 1670 and 1700 the white population of the English colonies doubled, while in the same period the number of blacks increased fivefold.

Americans joined in the enterprise, trading with African kings for what became more than nine million slaves. Some tried to rebel. In September 1739 about 75 slaves of Stono River country, near Charleston, stole weapons and with shouts of "Liberty!" set off for St. Augustine and a promise of freedom in Spanish territory. Before the militia suppressed the rebellion, 40 blacks and 20 whites died.

Shipping routes connected Britain with trading bases around the world. In a notorious link, British merchants sold iron and silver, finished goods, and textiles from British India to African kings and traders, who paid with slaves.

Between 1532 and 1870, more than 5.5 million slaves were imported into the Americas from Africa. Nearly 40 percent came from Angola, with large numbers coming from the bights of Benin and Biafra and Gold Coast. Nearly 3.6 million people were shipped to Portuguese Brazil, 1.6 million to the British Caribbean, 1.5 million to Spanish America, and some 400,000—about 6 percent—to British Colonial America. About two million African captives died at sea.

Nearly 40 percent of slaves that reached the British mainland colonies between 1700 and 1775 disembarked at Sullivan's Island,

OPPOSITE: *Slaves were crowded together aboard British slave ships, like the* Brookes, *during the Middle Passage.*

STOWAGE OF THE BRITISH SLAVE SHIP "BROOKES" UNDER THE

REGULATED SLAVE TRADE

Act of 1788.

Fig 1.
Longitudinal Section.

Note. The Brookes after the Regulation Act of 1788 was allowed to carry 454 Slaves. She could stow this number by following the rule adopted in this plate namely of allowing a space of 6 ft by 1 ft 4 In to each man, 5 ft 10 In by 11 ft 4 In to each woman & 5 ft by 1 ft 2 In to each boy, but so much space as this was seldom allowed or neater the Regulation Act It was proved by the confession of the Slave Merchant that before the above Act the Brookes had at one time carried as many as 609 Slaves. This was done by taking some out of Irons & locking them spoonwise to use the technical term; that is by stowing one within the distended legs of the other.

Poop

Captains Cabin

Gun Room

Hold for Provisions, Water &c.

Note. The shaded Squares indicate the beams of the Ship.

Shelf or Platform

Lower Deck

PLAN OF LOWER DECK WITH THE STOWAGE OF 292 SLAVES

130 OF THESE BEING STOWED <u>UNDER</u> THE SHELVES AS SHEWN IN FIGURE 6 & FIGURE 5.

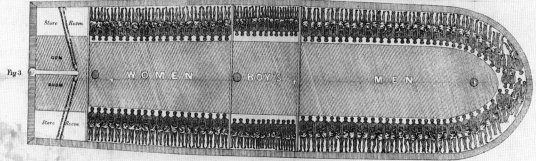

Fig 2.

Store Room

Store Room

PLAN SHEWING THE STOWAGE OF 130 ADDITIONAL SLAVES ROUND THE WINGS OR SIDES OF THE LOWER DECK BY MEANS OF PLATFORMS OR SHELVES
(IN THE MANNER OF GALLERIES IN A CHURCH) THE SLAVES STOWED <u>ON</u> THE SHELVES AND <u>BELOW</u> THEM HAVE ONLY A HEIGHT OF 2 FEET 7 INCHES
BETWEEN THE BEAMS: AND FAR LESS UNDER THE BEAMS. See Fig 1.

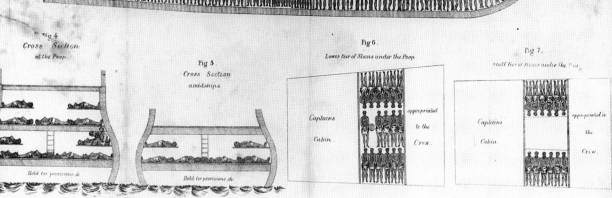

Fig 3.

Store Room

GUN

ROOM

Store Room

WOMEN   BOYS   MEN

Fig 4
Cross Section
at the Poop.

Fig 5.
Cross Section
amidships

Fig 6.
Lower tier of Slaves under the Poop.

Fig 7.
Shelf tier of Slaves under the Poop.

Hold for provisions &c

Hold for provisions &c

Captains Cabin.

appropriated to the Crew.

Captains Cabin.

appropriated to the Crew.

Scale of feet

Charleston. It was later described as the "Ellis Island of black Americans."

Farms that needed many workers—tobacco, rice, indigo—came to depend on slaves. By 1790 the slave population of the colonies was nearly 700,000, with 75 percent in the southern Atlantic states. By 1810, though all northern states had abolished slavery or provided for its end, 30,000 slaves worked there in fields, homes, and factories. The largest number, 15,017, labored in New York state under the harshest codes in the North. Twenty years later, Virginia still had the most slaves, but the spread of cotton into Alabama and Mississippi required massive increases in slave labor. The nation's slave population had grown to two million, and in the South more stringent codes were introduced to control and confine.

Josiah Henson was a slave until 1830, when he escaped to Canada. He described field-hand life: "The principal food . . . consisted of corn-meal, and salt herrings; to which was added in summer a little buttermilk, and the few vegetables . . . In ordinary times we had two regular meals in a day:—breakfast at twelve o'clock, after laboring from daylight, and supper when the work of the remainder of the day was over. In harvest season we had three . . . We lodged in log huts, and on the bare ground. Wooden floors were an unknown luxury. In a single room were huddled, like cattle, ten or a dozen persons, men, women and children . . . In these wretched hovels were we penned at night, and fed by day; here were the children born and the sick—neglected."

When the legal U.S. slave trade with Africa ended in 1808, domestic trading became big business in the South, where demand was growing as fast as the cotton. Finding less profit in owning slaves than in selling them, eastern farmers shipped slaves to the Gulf states. Most were auctioned at centers such as New Orleans, where a slave sold for a third more than in Virginia.

OPPOSITE: *A Union army guard stands in front of the Price, Birch, & Co Building, where slaves were once held, bought, and sold in Alexandria, Virginia.*

1750
THROUGH
1799

NEW PEOPLE *in a* NEW WORLD

I**N THE SECOND HALF OF THE 18TH** century, with Britain's attention often diverted by war with France, the American Colonies thrived during long stretches of virtual independence. When Britain demanded help with staggering war debts, the Americans saw the wisdom of common cause. Each British attempt to collect taxes forced the Colonies closer and broke another link to the mother country.

During these years, the Colonies' population grew, and borders were drawn; a flag was designed, and a capital city laid out on ten square miles of marshy land on the Potomac River in Maryland; George Washington evolved from being a tenacious and successful general to a higher status as Father of His Country; slaves were plentiful, and the colonists gradually began thinking of the Native Americans—the Indians—as the intruders and unlawful barriers to their plans and desires.

"The Revolution was effected before the war commenced. The Revolution was in the minds and hearts of the people," John Adams recalled. But minds and hearts couldn't govern a nation. Several years of loose confederation taught the need for a stronger central government. By 1788 the adoption of the new Constitution seemed to fulfill Samuel Adams's optimism of a decade earlier: "Our union is now complete; our constitution composed, established and approved. You are now the guardians of your own liberties."

The people's representatives grappled with issues that would extend into the 21st century: how to collect taxes, enforce laws, and get reelected while staying true to the Republic.

General George Washington and soldiers from the Continental Army parade as they enter New York City on November 25, 1783.

The FIRST COLONIES

Predecessors to the States

During the colonial period in North America, the British settlements grew so fast that by 1750, 13 separate colonies stretched from Maine to Georgia.

Farmers, fishermen, and craftsmen came to New England. "The air of the country is sharp," said a Massachusetts woman, "the rocks many, the trees innumerable, the grass little, the winter cold." It wouldn't be long before many of the New Englanders realized the area was not suitable for farming and turned to fishing, shipbuilding, or trade. The Pilgrims were the first English colonists to permanently settle in what is now Massachusetts. Their ship the *Mayflower* set off from Plymouth, England, in 1620, with 102 passengers. The Mayflower Compact, written and signed aboard the ship, set rules to guide the settlers in establishing a new community. It served as the official constitution of the Plymouth Colony for many years.

New Hampshire, aggressively explored by both the British and the French, was first settled by the English near Portsmouth in 1623 and named for Hampshire County in England. It shared a governor with Massachusetts until 1741.

Connecticut's first three permanent settlements—Hartford, Windsor, and Wethersfield, founded in 1635 and 1636—were established by colonists from Massachusetts Bay. In 1639 they adopted a constitution they called "Fundamental Orders," the first in the nation to be based on the consent of the governed; it later served as a model for the U.S. Constitution.

Rhode Island, never an island, was the smallest colony and is the smallest state. It was the first colony to declare independence but, worried that because of its small size it wouldn't be equitably represented, was the last to ratify the Constitution.

The temperate climate and richer soils of the middle colonies in the mid-Atlantic were better suited to farming. By 1624 the Dutch West India Company was exploring and settling in the New York region. Dutch settlers—one of them was Peter Minuit—bought Manhattan Island from local Indians and called it New Amsterdam. It became English in 1664.

Charles II made his brother James, Duke of York, proprietor of everything between the St. Croix and Delaware Rivers. James named the region after himself: New York. Some of the proprietors there in turn offered to sell parts of their holdings, publishing enticing advertisements.

CURRENCY OF THE COLONIES

The metal money of the 18th century in America was largely silver, not gold. The chief coin was the Spanish milled dollar—the piece of eight. There were some gold coins in circulation, however, especially the Johannes of Portugal, which circulated after 1722, and the Spanish Pistole, which had a substantial circulation in Virginia prior to the French and Indian War. The silver came largely through trade with the West Indies and the gold from trade with southern Europe. The colonies retained the British monetary units: pounds, shillings, and pence. Values were placed upon the coins by the colonial legislatures.

Paper currency was generally called "bills of credit" and was issued on two bases: on the credit of the colony supported by tax funds, and on loan, which meant a legislature printed a sum in bills and made them legal tender; these were then loaned, usually to landowners in the form of a mortgage on their land. Such currency gave individuals credit necessary for acquiring and improving land, and the interest they paid went into the public treasury. And the bills, while outstanding, supplied a medium of exchange. ∎

"There is so great an increase of grain," one boasted, "that within three years, some plantations have got 20 acres of corn . . . There are also peaches, in great quantities."

Pennsylvania might have been called just Sylvania, Quaker William Penn's first choice. He was granted a charter to the region in 1681. Its location in the middle of the arc of the 13 original colonies earned it a nickname: the Keystone State.

More than 90 Revolutionary War battles were fought in the colony of New Jersey, which was named for the Isle of Jersey in the English Channel. Delaware's first settlement by the Dutch was destroyed by Indians, and it became English in 1664. Leonard Calvert, son of Lord Baltimore, led the first group of settlers to Maryland in 1633. The colony was named for England's Queen Henrietta Maria, and its first capital was St. Mary's.

Virginia was the site of the first permanent English settlement in the New World—Jamestown—as well as the first popular assembly in America, convened in 1619. By 1653 Virginia

colonists were moving south to settle around Albemarle Sound, strengthening the colony's southern frontier. The name North Carolina first appeared in 1691, when the English crown officially recognized the region.

The Spanish reached the South Carolina region as early as 1514 and the French attempted settlement in 1562. South Carolina was the first state to secede from the Union in 1860, one of the triggers that launched the Civil War.

Georgia, the last colony to be settled, was named for King George II and granted in 1732 to one of his generals, James Oglethorpe. It was hoped that Georgia would slow the encroachment of Spanish and French settlers from the south.

ABOVE: *The finest depiction of the colonies in 1755, John Mitchell's map was drafted for the Lords Commissioners for Trade and Plantations.*
NEXT: *Tall ships stand in the harbor of Mystic Seaport in Connecticut, first settled in 1614 by the Dutch.*

The REVOLUTIONARY WAR

Seeds of Unrest

By 1700, England's mainland colonies were thriving. Their population stood at 250,000 people and would quadruple by mid-century. Colonists were growing prosperous on agriculture. In New England, yeomen owned their land. Land ownership was "what chiefly induces people into America," said a New York official. English ships bound for world markets were filled with tobacco from Virginia and Maryland and rice from the Carolinas. Ships from New England carried produce to the British West Indies. Colonists were required by Parliament to ship some commodities—including tobacco—to Britain, which sold them in Europe for nice profits. By 1750 American products accounted for a third of Britain's export trade. But American merchants were finding ways to evade British laws. The British policy of "salutary neglect" regulated only defense and trade, so elected assemblies in each colony assumed the powers to make laws and levy taxes. Royal governors retained veto powers, but assemblies had the authority to withhold their pay.

The colonies set up advisory assemblies with the authority to levy taxes and pay officials. And with Britain's attention often diverted by war with France, the colonies thrived during long stretches of virtual independence. When war broke out once again with France in the 1750s, Britain demanded the colonies' help with the huge war debts. But each demand for more taxes strained the colonies' relationship with England.

At the same time, American merchants were trading illegally with French Caribbean sugar islands. The British resolved to reassert control. Customs agents were ordered to crack down on and courts to try smugglers. For the first time,

Britain posted a large peacetime army in the American colonies.

In 1774, the British Parliament closed Boston Harbor after colonial agitators, called the Sons of Liberty, dumped British-owned tea into the harbor. Britain was attempting to make the colonies shoulder part of the tremendous expenses and debts of maintaining troops in the new territories, but Americans, accustomed by now to governing and taxing themselves, saw no reason to pay. Various money-raising acts—the Sugar Act of 1764, the Stamp Act of 1765, the Townshend

---

THE FIRST SUBMARINE

An unlikely craft saw service in the American Revolution. *The Turtle*, a watertight oak submarine designed and built by David Bushnell, was the first submarine used during warfare. The barrel-shaped craft held one person and was propelled by a handcrank. It could descend or rise by admitting and releasing water into ballast tanks. It had enough air to last half an hour. Its mission was to submerge beneath a British ship and force a long screw into the ship's hull. A watertight cask filled with gunpowder would then be attached to the screw and a fuse ignited.

The Turtle launched itself against a British warship anchored in the New York Harbor on September 6, 1776. Army sergeant Ezra Lee was at the controls. But the submarine's screw hit an iron plate and was unable to penetrate the hull. *The Turtle* made two more unsuccessful attempts before being retired. But it won fame as the first submarine to be used in a military operation. ■

ABOVE: *On March 5, 1770, British soldiers and Boston citizens fought in "The Boston Massacre," shown in this sensationalized depiction published by Paul Revere.*

Acts of 1767—spurred American defiance. "The cause of Boston," said George Washington, "the despotick measures in respect to it, I mean, now is and ever will be considered as the cause of America."

Colonists sent delegates to congresses in 1765, 1774, and 1775; committees of correspondence traded news. John Adams and other leaders argued that Parliament could not pass laws that violated

Americans' "essential rights as British subjects," such as trial by jury and taxation only if accompanied by representation. Positions on both sides hardened, and rhetoric grew inflammatory. In 1775, George III and his ministers vowed to master the "unhappy and deluded multitude" of Americans.

Force "should be repelled by force," the British government commanded Gen. Thomas Gage when New England began raising troops. On April 18, 1775, Gage sent troops from Boston to Concord, Massachusetts. Warned by Paul Revere, 70 militiamen met 180 British soldiers at Lexington on April 19. The forces exchanged shots, and the redcoats marched on to Concord, where 450 Americans faced 700 British. Americans lined the roads to Boston, firing continually from behind houses, barns, trees, and stone walls. By day's end, 49 Americans and 73 British had been killed.

Early battles raged around Boston. There some 3,000 colonists amassed to loosen the British grip on Boston. Gen. William Howe, the British commander, ordered a traditional frontal attack on June 17, 1775. The Americans succeeded in repelling the 2,300 redcoats twice but retreated after running out of ammunition. Technically a British victory, the battle—misnamed for nearby Bunker Hill—killed 226 redcoats and boosted American morale.

Thomas Paine's tract, "Common Sense," rallied the colonists: "Everything that is right or reasonable pleads for separation. The blood of the slain, the weeping voice of nature cries, Tis time to part." The pamphlet sold 120,000 copies in 1776 and, according to George Washington, worked "a powerful change in the minds of men." On July 4, 1776, delegates from each colony approved the Declaration of Independence. John Adams brooded about the "bloody conflict we are destined to endure."

American spirits were buoyed by news that at Christmastime, 1776, Washington took a

thousand British and Hessian prisoners at Trenton, New Jersey. Britain possessed the world's largest navy, but its small professional army was no match for the Colonials. The British lost an entire army at Saratoga, New York, in 1777.

After the failed British offensive in Massachusetts and disastrous American forays into Canada, the war shifted to the mid-Atlantic. Defeats did not discourage Washington, who by 1778 acknowledged a standoff: "Both armies are brought back to the very point they set out from." Also in 1778, seven states signed the Articles of Confederation, and France declared war against Great Britain. But a joint campaign of American troops under Gen. John Sullivan and the French fleet of Count Jean Baptiste d'Estaing failed to take British-held Newport, Rhode Island.

The American situation was not helped by the dithering of the Continental Congress, which hesitated to exercise its power and failed to raise sufficient sums through taxation. Soldiers often went without pay. Managing the war itself fell largely on Washington, but the longer he managed to keep his ragged troops in the field, the more war weariness grew in Britain. The French alliance with the colonists in 1778 and loans from European bankers further helped the cause for American independence.

Late in 1778 Britain looked to the South to find "good Americans to subdue the bad ones." A British army led by Lord Cornwallis instead found guerrilla war and mounting casualties. Harried by Gen. Nathanael Greene, Cornwallis turned north to Virginia, which he considered pivotal in training and supplying American troops. His surrender at Yorktown ended Britain's southern strategy—and effectively ended the war.

In August 1782, Britain and the Continental Army clashed in South Carolina, their last battle in the East, and the next year the Continental Army disbanded, though a contingent stayed on duty until all British troops had withdrawn.

The war's end did not usher in unanimity among Americans. When the British left, so did much of the Americans' sense of common cause.

PAUL REVERE'S RIDE
by HENRY WADSWORTH LONGFELLOW

Listen my children and you shall hear
Of the midnight ride of Paul Revere
On the eighteenth of April, in Seventy-five;...
He said to his friend, "If the British march
By land or sea from the town to-night,
Hang a lantern aloft in the belfry arch
Of the North Church tower as a signal light,—
One if by land, and two if by sea;
And I on the opposite shore will be,...
Now he patted his horse's side,
Now he gazed at the landscape far and near,
Then, impetuous, stamped the earth,
And turned and tightened his saddle girth;...
And lo! as he looks, on the belfry's height
A glimmer, then a gleam of light!
He springs to the saddle,...
A hurry of hoofs in a village street,
A shape in the moonlight, a bulk in the dark,
And beneath, from the pebbles,
in passing, a spark
Struck out by a steed flying fearless and fleet;...
It was two by the village clock,
When he came to the bridge in Concord town.
He heard the bleating of the flock,
And the twitter of birds among the trees,
You know the rest. In the books you have read
How the British Regulars fired and fled,—
A cry of defiance, and not of fear,
A voice in the darkness, a knock at the door,
And a word that shall echo for evermore!
For, borne on the night-wind of the Past,
Through all our history, to the last,
In the hour of darkness and peril and need,
The people will waken and listen to hear
The hurrying hoof-beats of that steed,
And the midnight message of Paul Revere.

LEFT: *Percy Moran painted this depiction of George Washington and his troops during the brutal winter of 1777–1778 at Valley Forge, Pennsylvania.*

DECLARATION *of* INDEPENDENCE

First Steps to Freedom

On a day that would become forever sacred to Americans, July 4, 1776, the Continental Congress, gathered in Philadelphia, declared to the world that the Colonies were separating from their mother country, Great Britain. They issued a Declaration of Independence that set out the arguments why "these United Colonies" should be free and independent. Writing for the U.S. National Archives, Professor Stephen E. Lucas has called the Declaration "perhaps the most masterfully written state paper of Western civilization."

Before the fighting against Britain's forces began on April 19, 1775, most colonists favored continued union with the mother country. But as the fighting dragged on, and as Britain's forces in North America grew ever larger and more intrusive, most people came to favor separation.

At the Continental Congress, Thomas Jefferson, John Adams, Benjamin Franklin, Roger Sherman, and Robert R. Livingston were named to a committee to draft a statement, setting out the reasons for independence. In turn, the committee chose Jefferson to write the first draft. Franklin and Adams read the document and made a few changes. It was presented to the full congress, which passed it.

John Dunlap, official printer to the Congress, worked through the night. On July 5, copies were dispatched to various assemblies, conventions, as

well as to the commanders of Continental troops. There are 24 copies known to exist today.

But the Declaration had not yet become the iconic image prominent in American history books. On July 19, Congress ordered the Declaration to be "fairly engrossed on parchment, with the title and stile of 'The unanimous declaration of the thirteen United States of America,' and that the same, when engrossed, be signed by every member of Congress." An embosser, perhaps Timothy Matlack, though no one is quite certain, created the handsome document, with its flowing calligraphy, that is so familiar today. On August 2 the document was ready for signing. John Hancock went first, with a flourish; the other delegates followed. As was standard procedure in the day, their signatures are spaced on the document according to the geographic location of their states: New Hampshire appears at the top of the list and Georgia at the bottom. Though 56 delegates signed, two demurred: John Dickinson, still hopeful of reconciliation with Britain, and Robert R. Livingston, who thought it too soon for such a declaration.

ABOVE: *Benjamin Franklin, John Adams, and Thomas Jefferson draft the Declaration of Independence.*
RIGHT: *An 1896 facsimile of the Declaration is decorated with images of all the signers around the border.*

DECLARATION · OF · INDEPENDENCE

DEVELOPMENT *of the*
POLITICAL PARTIES

~

Federalists and Republicans

After the Revolution was over, the former Colonies had to decide how to organize themselves into a new nation. In 1781, the Articles of Confederation were ratified by the states, but this loose system of government was too weak to succeed. Congress could not tax citizens directly, which resulted in a lack of funds to pay government expenses, the public debt, or the armed forces.

AARON BURR

Grandson of the theologian Jonathan Edwards, Aaron Burr was orphaned at a young age when illness took both his parents. Raised by his uncle, he studied law before leaving to fight in the Continental Army during the American Revolution, during which he served on the staff of General Washington.

After the war, Burr embarked on a successful legal and political career. He served as senator from New York and became vice president in 1800. Burr is probably most famous for his duel with rival Alexander Hamilton. In 1804 Burr ran unsuccessfully for the governorship of New York; Hamilton had worked against Burr's campaign by writing and saying derogatory things about him. Because of Hamilton's actions, Burr challenged him to a duel. The two met on July 11, 1804, in Weehawken, New Jersey. Hamilton was mortally wounded and died the next day. Charged with murder, Burr left the state. He would return to Washington, D.C., to finish his term as vice president and thus end his political career.

Burr next embarked on a series of adventures in the West. The most notorious were the alleged plans to create his own nation from lands in the Louisiana Purchase. For this, Burr was arrested, charged with treason, and acquitted by Chief Justice John Marshall. ■

Among the Founding Fathers, a movement to strengthen the central government began to grow. George Washington, John Jay, and Alexander Hamilton were among the strongest advocates for a stronger federal government, one that could levy taxes and raise funds. But some Americans wanted to keep the states powerful; they preferred a weak central state. These two philosophies would shape the creation of the United States Constitution and the Bill of Rights. Their debates would remerge after its ratification in 1789 in the first two-party system of the United States.

President Washington felt that political parties would harm the new nation and warned citizens against them. After his two-term presidency ended in 1796, he said, "I have already intimated to you the danger of parties in the State . . . Let me now . . . warn you in the most solemn manner against the baneful effects of the spirit of party . . . It serves always to distract the public councils and enfeeble the public administration. It agitates the community with ill-founded jealousies and false alarms; kindles the animosity of one part against another; foments occasionally riot and insurrection. It opens the door to foreign influence and corruption, which finds a facilitated access to the government itself through the channels of party passion."

Despite Washington's warnings, two political parties emerged: the Federalists, led by Alexander Hamilton, and the Republicans, led by Thomas Jefferson. The Federalists favored a strong central government and the development of industry, while the Republicans favored an agrarian-based society and a weaker government.

The text within the map image includes:

Breadth of the Streets.
THE Grand avenue and such Streets as lead immediately to public places are from 130 to 160 feet wide and may be conveniently divided into foot ways walks of trees and a carriage way. The other Streets are from 90 to 110 feet Wide

The Water of Tiber Creek may be conveyed on the high ground where the Capitol stands and after watering that part of the City may be delivered to other useful Purposes. The Perpendicular height of the ground where the Capitol is to stand, is above the tide of Tiber Creek 70 Feet

PLAN of the City of Washington in the Territory of Columbia ceded by the States of VIRGINIA and MARYLAND to the United States of America and by them established as the SEAT of their GOVERNMENT after the Year MDCCC.

GEORGE TOWN

Latitude Capitol. 38.53.N.

Longitude. 0.0.

Observations explanatory of the Plan.

POTOMAK RIVER

PART OF VIRGINIA WITHIN THE TERRITORY OF COLUMBIA

EASTERN BRANCH

PART OF MARYLAND WITHIN THE TERRITORY OF COLUMBIA

SCALE OF POLES.

Jefferson's supporters benefited from internal strife within the Federalist party during John Adams's presidency (1797–1801). Hamilton and Adams vied for control of the party, while heated conflicts arose over American attitudes to the French Revolution as well as Hamilton's fiscal policies. Divisions within the party hurt the Federalists and ultimately cost them the presidency in the election of 1800. After John Adams's administration ended, the Federalists would never regain the presidency and their former political power.

The Democratic-Republican candidates, Thomas Jefferson and Aaron Burr, won the election of 1800. Their party dominated national politics for the next 30 years. When Jefferson took office, he used his inaugural address to heal the wounds caused by political factions. He said: "We have called by different names brethren of the same principle. We are all Republicans, we are all Federalists. . . . I believe this . . . the strongest Government on earth . . . Let us, then, with courage and confidence pursue our own Federal and Republican principles, our attachment to union and representative government."

ABOVE: *The city plan of Washington, D.C., was criss-crossed by broad avenues. This version from 1792 appeared on a souvenir handkerchief.*

The COTTON GIN

~

Machine of Slavery

Early cotton plantations in the South flourished along the coast, where they grew a long-fibered cotton that could be easily separated from the seed. But this type of cotton could be grown only in a small coastal area, so inland planters could not rely on cotton as a cash crop.

Inland farmers grew a green-seeded, or short-staple, cotton, a variety hardy enough to survive winters. To an 18th-century grower, it was "so full of Seeds, that it cannot be cleansed by the ordinary Way of a Gin, or by any other Means than picking out with Fingers." Most of the cotton was grown on plantations, cultivated and picked by slaves. The job of seeding cotton by hand was enormously time-consuming. A young

---

"COTTON IS KING"
MARCH 4, 1858

But if there were no other reason why we should never have war, would any sane nation make war on cotton? Without firing a gun, without drawing a sword, should they make war on us we could bring the whole world to our feet. The South is perfectly competent to go on, one, two, or three years without planting a seed of cotton. I believe that if she was to plant but half her cotton, for three years to come, it would be an immense advantage to her. I am not so sure but that after three years' entire abstinence she would come out stronger than ever she was before, and better prepared to enter afresh upon her great career of enterprise. What would happen if no cotton was furnished for three years? I will not stop to depict what every one can imagine, but this is certain: England would topple headlong and carry the whole civilized world with her, save the South. No, you dare not make war on cotton. No power on earth dares to make war upon it. Cotton is king.

–James Henry Hammond
Senator from South Carolina

Yale graduate named Eli Whitney solved the problem, and his invention helped to spread cotton plantations and slavery throughout the South. By 1820 the cotton frontier had pushed westward from the coastal regions into parts of Tennessee, Alabama, Mississippi, and Louisiana.

Eli Whitney was born in 1765 on a farm near Westborough, Massachusetts. At age 18, Whitney became a schoolteacher. After teaching for five years, he departed for New Haven and Yale.

College broadened Whitney's outlook, stimulated his already active mind, and smoothed his country manners. It also introduced him to contacts who would be important to him as a businessman throughout his life. He graduated intending to study law and engaged himself as a tutor to a South Carolina planter's family. The tutoring job fell through.

While journeying south Whitney had met Catherine Greene, widow of the late Gen. Nathanael Greene, her children, and her estate manager. Their friendship blossomed, and Mrs. Green invited Whitney to stay at her plantation near Savannah, Georgia, as her guest. Within two weeks of his arrival in 1793 he had invented the machine that made his fame.

It was simplicity itself. Slender wire fingers, picking up cotton fed into a curved hopper, carried the fibers through a grid at the top that was too fine for seeds, which fell away. "The cotton is put into the Hopper," he wrote, "carried thro' the Breastwork by the teeth, brushed off from the teeth by the Clearer and flies off from the Clearer with the assistance of the air, by its own centrifugal force. The machine is turned by water, horses or in any other way as is most convenient.

The machinery was so simple that farmers found they could make their own, and Whitney spent years fighting to protect his patent and for a share of the wealth from cotton. He managed to pursuade several states to pay him a flat fee for the right to use his machine, but he barely covered expenses before his patent expired in 1807.

Cotton farming mushroomed. In 1795 planters grew eight million pounds; 12 years later the crop had increased to 80 million pounds, thanks largely to Whitney's gin. Cotton became king. But its rapid spread also led to an explosion in the number of slaves in the United States: from fewer than 700,000 slaves in 1790 to more than two million 40 years later. Whitney's invention revolutionized cotton farming, but it also prolonged the barbaric institution of slavery.

At about the same time that the Whitney gin was catching on, the newly mechanized British textile industry was increasing its demand for U.S. cotton. Two million pounds of raw cotton were sent to Europe in 1794; 62 million were sent in 1811. Southern cotton growers could meet the demand largely because of Whitney's cotton gin.

By 1811 Whitney himself was a bitter man. He wrote to fellow inventor Robert Fulton: "this Machine being immensely profitable to almost every individual in the Country all were interested in trespassing, & each justified & kept the other in countenance."

By early in the 18th century, growing waves of immigrants were arriving on America's shores. Many found work in mills that made thread and cloth. Such mills used up enormous quantities of raw cotton, which by 1850 became firmly established as America's most valuable crop.

BELOW: *Huge demand for cotton had to be met by slaves and sharecroppers alike. Here, black sharecroppers work a Tennessee cotton field around 1899.*

1800
THROUGH
1849

FORMING *a* MORE PERFECT UNION

VICTORY IN THE REVOLUTIONARY WAR brought the United States a vast western domain, as Virginia, New York, and Connecticut abandoned claims to land northwest of the Ohio River. But Indian strength impeded settlement by American settlers. After settling land disputes with New York, Vermont became the first state added to the original 13. Virginia's western district of Kentucky gained statehood a year later.

After victory at Yorktown, the young United States found themselves with an enormous national debt, millions of dollars owed to France and to private citizens. With no authorization to levy taxes, the Confederation Congress looked to land sales for revenues. Land it had in abundance—the public domain, swaths of land stretching to the Mississippi River. This land could be disposed of for money, and as the country grew westward, more vast stretches of public domain became available.

A grid of geometric square-mile sections would pattern the growing United States. Surveying had its beginnings in the Land Ordinance of 1785, which empowered a national geographer to direct the survey of lands purchased from the Indians northwest of the Ohio River. By 1796 the grid system was standard and eased westward expansion.

But expansion into the West was fraught with disagreements over the future of slavery. Some states wished to expand the inhuman practice into new states while others wanted it ended forever. The conflict grew during this era, and would explode in the next.

Heart of New Orleans: the Vieux Carré and its bustling waterfront, ca 1885, was nurtured by trade traveling along the Mississippi River.

The LOUISIANA PURCHASE

~

Bargain of the Century

In 1801, when people spoke of Louisiana they meant, roughly, the mid part of North America encompassed by the drainage systems of the Missouri River and the southwestern tributaries of the Mississippi River. It was an enormous territory, claimed by Spain; though, except for a handful of garrisons on the Mississippi, in St. Louis, and in New Orleans, there were few

---

TOUSSAINT L'OUVERTURE

A teetotaling, vegetarian son of a slave born in 1743 on the island of Santo Domingo played a crucial role in the successful acquisition of the Louisiana Territory by the U.S.

As a youth Toussaint L'Ouverture learned to speak some French and impressed a plantation manager to the point that he was made a steward. He became a devout Catholic and in 1791 joined a rebellion of slaves in the northern province. He became so disillusioned with its leadership he formed an army of his own; they trained in guerrilla warfare. His authority and strength increased steadily, and by 1801 he commanded the forces of the entire island. Napoleon confirmed him in power but at the same time distrusted him; Toussaint loved France, but was frightened of Napoleon. He became somewhat paranoid, unsure of himself, weary of warfare. To regain control, France invaded the island in 1802, and most white citizens were happy to see the French troops. After a few months of fighting, Toussaint surrendered. But the same year, the French, suspecting him of plotting an uprising, arrested him and sent him to Fort de Joux in the French Alps. He was imprisoned there until his death in April 1803.

But his resistance had nearly bankrupted Napoleon, who sold Louisiana largely to help finance his army. ∎

Spaniards there to hold onto it. The Spaniards also claimed the whole of the Pacific Coast, though Russians had settled around the mouth of the Columbia River. And the Oregon country west of the Rocky Mountains, sprinkled with British fur traders, was claimed by England. The French, especially the trappers, had seen more of Louisiana than anyone else, and they seemed to be the only Europeans with much interest in it.

In 1801, Thomas Jefferson was worried by news from Europe in 1801. Napoleon Bonaparte, determined to rebuild a French colonial empire in North America, had, through the Treaty of San Ildefonso in 1800, persuaded the Spanish to "retrocede" the port of New Orleans and all the territory of Louisiana west of the Mississippi to France. Jefferson knew very well what this meant: Instead of a weak Spanish government in America's West there would be a French one. And the French were, at the time, the most powerful military force in the world.

In a bold move, Jefferson set out to buy Louisiana from France. His minister there, Robert R. Livingston, was directed to open negotiations—but only for New Orleans, through whose port most of the nation's produce passed, and for the colonies of eastern and western Florida.

Jefferson received another piece of bad news in 1802: Spanish officials in New Orleans had withdrawn the United States' "right of deposit," which meant American merchants could no longer store goods waiting to be shipped in the city. They wanted action.

Coincidentally, Napoleon was having troubles of his own. His island colony on Santo Domingo was in open rebellion. The French force there, the

The PRAIRIE DOG sickened at the sting of the HORNET
or a Diplomatic Puppet exhibiting his Deceptions!

force that would be used to occupy Louisiana, had been routed from the island by a combination of yellow fever and guerrilla warfare.

Jefferson moved on two fronts. He sent James Monroe to France to assist Livingston with the negotiations. And he quietly sent a message to Congress proposing an expedition into the West, calling it a "literary pursuit." He emphasized the commercial advantages, noting the "great supplies of furs & pelty" that could be trapped in the region. He sought and was granted $2,500 "for the purpose of extending the external commerce of the U.S."

Meanwhile, in France, Napoleon was losing interest in Louisiana. He had lost 50,000 French lives in Santo Domingo and had concluded that Louisiana wasn't worth the trouble or the money. "I renounce Louisiana," he said. But he didn't want the territory to fall into the hands of his hated enemies, the British. To have it under U.S. control would be "more useful to the policy and even to the commerce of France." He would sell the Americans the entire territory.

Neither Monroe, who arrived in Paris the next day, nor Livingston had the authority for such a purchase. To buy territory that would in effect double the size of the U.S. far exceeded their warrant. But there was no time to send to America for instructions. With breathtaking audacity, they accepted the offer.

Napoleon, too, was delighted with the deal. "The sale assures forever the power of the United States," he said, "and I have given England a rival who, sooner or later, will humble her pride."

Under the American flag now came more than 830,000 square miles of new territory—for 15 million dollars, less than three cents an acre. And with Louisiana in American hands, Jefferson was more determined than ever to have the new territory explored. He immediately turned his attention to organizing an expedition.

ABOVE: *The Louisiana Purchase is mocked by a cartoonist. Napoleon, a hornet, stings Jefferson, a prairie dog, causing him to "cough up" two million dollars.*

LEWIS *and* CLARK

Exploring the West

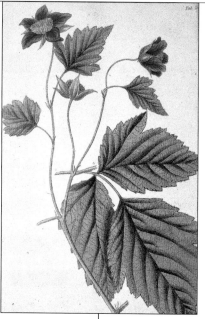

President Thomas Jefferson had long hungered for knowledge about that part of the North American continent that lay beyond the Alleghenies. He got Congress to finance an exploratory expedition there and chose his personal secretary Meriwether Lewis to lead it; Lewis called upon an old friend and colleague, William Clark, to be his co-captain.

Their instructions from Jefferson were lengthy and precise: to collect information both scientific and practical about the land, soil, geology, flora and fauna, even what he called "useful" plants and animals. They were to explore the possibility of engaging in friendly relations with the western Indian tribes.

Lewis and Clark decided between themselves to share command as well as the title "Captain" and devoted some months to putting together a party of about 25 frontiersmen, soldiers, and French trappers who had some knowledge of the West. They drew supplies from the army depot at Harpers Ferry. For food they packed flour, pork, a hundred gallons of whiskey, salt, and corn. They took 14 bales of beads and tobacco and ribbon and fishhooks for trading with the Indians. To help them map the countryside, they carried a sextant and chronometer, telescope and quadrant.

They pushed off up the muddy Missouri River in May 1804. They would traverse a total of 8,000 miles between St. Louis and the Pacific Ocean. They would impress many of the Indian tribes they met with the inevitable growth of the United States, an entity of which the Indians had never

heard. They would fight biting winds and clouds of "musquitrs and knats" but would persevere.

They called themselves the Corps of Discovery. Included in the party were a Newfoundland retriever named Seaman and Clark's African American slave, York. In the first winter, the Corps would grow to include a young Indian girl. Her name— Sacagawea—translates as Bird Woman. For many years legend gave her more credit than she actually deserved, calling her the expedition's guide and describing her as pointing the way West. She didn't do those things, but she did add measurably to the success of the expedition. She served as interpreter with her people, the Shoshone, during crucial negotiations for horses and guides to cross the mountains. Lewis praised her "fortitude and resolution." Perhaps most important, she reassured potentially hostile tribes of Indians by her mere presence: War parties were seldom accompanied by women.

Both captains and several of the other men kept journals of the journey. Clark was the worse speller but the more conscientious diarist; long gaps exist in Lewis's journals.

During the hot summer of 1804 the men battled the strong Missouri current across today's Missouri and along the border between Iowa and Nebraska. The heat and the mosquitoes bothered them greatly: "Muskuitors verry troublesom," Clark wrote. One man got "snakebit," but recovered.

Jefferson's instructions to them had included orders to observe "the face of the country, its growth & vegetable productions . . . the animals of the country generally, & especially those not known in the U.S." They logged careful observations of plants and animals that were new to them into their journals, and by the journey's end they had described hundreds of species previously unknown to science. They were the first to describe the grizzly bear, the black-tailed prairie dog, the white-tailed jackrabbit, the Missouri beaver, the sage grouse, the western rattler and western tanager, the cottonwood, and the mountain goat. They lost many of their plant specimens when water seeped into a cache but still managed to bring back 200 gathered between Great Falls, Missouri, and the Pacific coast.

It took them two and a half months to reach the vicinity of present-day Council Bluffs, where they met with some Otoe and Missouri Indians. Nearby, on August 20, Sergeant Charles Floyd died. Incredibly, he was the only casualty the party would suffer during the entire journey.

They spent their first winter among the Mandan Indians near present-day Bismarck, North Dakota. There, they built Fort Mandan, a wooden stockade, and settled in. During the long dark winter the captains prepared an interim report for Jefferson, and packed Indian artifacts and scientific specimens to send back to him in the spring. When spring arrived they set off up the river once more, in two pirogues—a sort of flat-bottomed dugout—and six canoes that the

SEAMAN

"Very active strong and docile," Lewis wrote of his Newfoundland dog Seaman. He would prove himself to be all those things during the trip to the Pacific and back. Lewis bought him for $20 in the East and, during the trip up the Missouri, Seaman retrieved a goose, finished off a deer a hunter had wounded, and caught beaver, even diving into their lodges. Near the mouth of the Yellowstone he caught an antelope in midstream and brought it ashore. One night while the camp slept, Seaman barked to turn aside a buffalo bull lurching toward camp and the sleeping men.

With his heavy coat, Seaman suffered from the summer heat, and a wounded beaver bit his leg, severing an artery and nearly killing him. The bugs and prickly-pear cactus that tormented the men also tormented him.

They named a creek after him—Seaman Creek, now Monture Creek—a swift stream that flows into the Blackfoot River. ■

BELOW: *Using compass readings taken on the outward trek, Clark drew accurate maps of Western topography.*
OPPOSITE: *A drawing of the salmonberry, depicted by Lewis and Clark in their journals.*

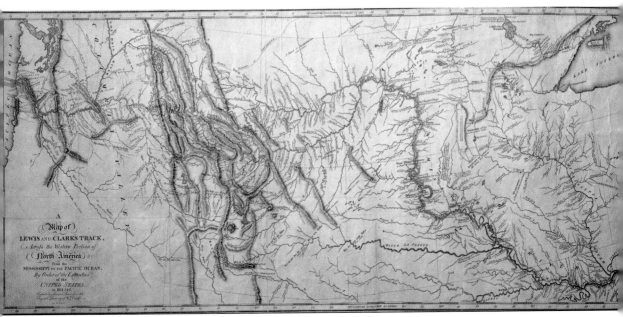

A Map of LEWIS AND CLARK'S TRACK, Across the Western Portion of North America from the MISSISSIPPI TO THE PACIFIC OCEAN; By Order of the Executive of the UNITED STATES in 1804.5.6.

the under shell. the animal is soft & boneless. —

The white salmon Trout which we had previously

en only at the great falls of the Columbia, has

ow made its appearance in the creeks near

is place. one of them was brought us to

ay by an Indian who had just

ken it with his gig. this is a

kenep of it; it was 2 feet 8 Inches

ng, and weighed 10 lb. the eye

ately large, the pupile

ith a small admixture of yellow, and

d iris of a silvery white,

bid near it's border with

mn. the position

ay be seen from

y are small

the fish. the fins

inted except the

ich are a

ck fin and

in each

ls

lve,

on the

ys, but

ered with

oportion

tongue

k

is ma

black

is a little

a yellowis

of the fin

the drawing

in proportion

are boney but n

tail and back fe

little so. the prin

ventral ones, co

ten rays; those of the

thirteen, that of the tail

and the small fin placed

tail above has no bony

is a tough flexable substance

smooth skin. it is thicker in

to its width than the salmon.

is thick and firm beset on each border

small subulate teeth in a single series.

the teeth of the mouth are as before dis

cribed. neither this fish nor the salmon

men had made during the winter. Lewis wrote, "We were now about to penetrate a country at least two thousand miles in width . . . the good or evil it had in store for us was . . . yet to determine."

They devoted several weeks to portaging around the Great Falls of the Missouri—five cataracts within 12 miles, now largely lost behind dams. It was a hot 16-mile portage, across endless stretches of prickly-pear cactus whose spines penetrated their moccasins. The falls, "hising flashing and sparkling" in their path, were one of the greatest obstacles they would face.

It had been reported to them that a portage of just 20 miles separated the headwaters of the Missouri from those of the Columbia. Instead they found 220 miles of "high mountain countrey thickley covered with pine." By early summer they could see the glitter of snow on distant mountains to the north and west, mountains they would have to cross. They were discouraged to find that "the adjacent mountains commonly rise so high as to concel the more distant . . . from our view." Here were the massive ranges of the American Rocky Mountains.

They pressed on. They reached a place where the river forked into three branches. They named them for Gallatin, Madison, and Jefferson and followed the Jefferson to the Missouri's headwaters. But now they needed to cross the mountains before another winter set in. They were counting on Sacagawea, who had been born nearby—she had been kidnapped by a rival tribe as a child—to negotiate for horses and guides. And when they finally found some Indians, an amazing coincidence was revealed. Sacagawea "came into the tent, sat down, and was beginning to interpret, when in the person of [the chief] she recognized her brother: She instantly jumped up, and ran and embraced him, throwing over him her blanket and weeping profusely." The Corps of Discovery had stumbled upon the very band from which she had been stolen.

The Corps set off across the Bitterroot Mountains. The autumn snows began. They passed "up & Down Steep hills, where Several horses fell, Some turned over, and others Sliped down . . . one horse Crippeled & 2 gave out." They melted snow for water and, as food supplies ran lower and lower, subsisted on dehydrated soup and bear's oil. "I have been wet and as cold in every part as I ever was in my life," wrote Clark.

But on September 19, Clark looked westward from a peak and saw an "emence Plain and leavel Countrey." They were across the worst of the mountains. They built more canoes, this time from huge pine trees, and took to the water once again, this time traveling with the current. They replenished their food from friendly Nez Percé Indians. They floated the Clearwater to the Snake, the Snake to the Columbia, the Columbia to the ocean. On October 21, they met an Indian wearing a "Salors Jacket" and a week later "Great numbers of Sea Otters." At the mouth of the Columbia, as fall progressed, they began building another fort where they would spend their second winter. They called it Fort Clatsop after a local tribe of Indians.

By early spring they were eager to start for home. By September 1806, they came floating down to a tumultuous welcome in St. Louis. "Never did a similar event excite more joy thro' the United States," wrote a relieved Jefferson on their return. He was delighted with the information they brought him. Their diaries catalogued 122 new species and subspecies of birds, fish, amphibians, mammals, and reptiles; and nearly 200 plants, many of them edible or medicinal.

Jefferson was disappointed with two pieces of information: There was no "practicable water communication across this continent for the purposes of commerce," as he had hoped. And there was no evidence of an ice-free Northwest Passage.

Still, the explorers brought back information about the American West that would lure more explorers and finally settlers. And their successful trip would give the U.S. a strong advantage as it laid claim to the Pacific Northwest.

LEFT: *Meticulous in their quest for knowledge of the natural world, Lewis and Clark made extensive notes and drawings of the flora and fauna of the new West. From the Columbia River came a eulachon, or candlefish.*

TRADE *on the* WUATER

The Canals and the Mississippi

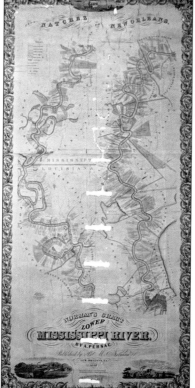

Before steamboats and railroads, canals successfully provided transport in the U.S. At their height, a score of canals veined the East with 4,000 miles of waterways. Settlers could travel for a penny and a half per mile on the Erie Canal in 1825, while the cost of moving a ton of freight from Albany to Buffalo dropped from $100 by wagon to $20 by barge and the time from 20 days to 8 days. Settlers in the Midwest could ship a hundred times more coal or wheat on a canal boat than on a wagon, and the load could be hauled twice as far in a day with the same number of horses it took to pull the wagon.

Treasury Secretary Albert Gallatin had proposed a national plan of canals and roads as early as 1808. Construction began at Rome, New York, on the Erie Canal, on the Fourth of July, 1817. The mammoth project was designed to connect the Atlantic seaboard with the Great Lakes.

The canal was 40 feet wide, 4 feet deep, and 363 miles long. In October 1825, the last link was dug and the buoyant governor, aboard the canalboat Seneca Chief, led a ceremonial flotilla from Lake Erie to New York Harbor. Fireworks exploded from canalside towns as the boats passed. New York used a combination of techniques for financing the canal: sale of canal stocks, tolls, and taxes on salt and auctions. It was so successful that a frenzy of canal building began throughout the states, producing 3,326 miles of canals by 1840.

By 1852 canals were hauling nine million tons of freight, and just before the Civil War 188 million dollars had been invested in canals. The 395-mile-long Main Line passed through Pennsylvania and crossed the Allegheny Mountains; a cable railroad carried the canalboats over the mountains. The longest of the canals, the Wabash and Erie, stretched for 468 miles. Canals were useful to the public for shipping goods, but the coming of the railroad spelled their doom.

In the West, rivers were the main arteries for exploration and trade. First proved commercially feasible in 1807 by Robert Fulton, steamboats fanned out on the Ohio, Mississippi, Missouri, Red, and Arkansas Rivers. With serviceable roads few and far between, the West was blessed with a network of long, navigable rivers: the Mississippi and Missouri, along with their hundreds of miles of navigable tributaries.

The arrival of steamboats on the Mississippi River in 1811 revolutionized trade and communications. Robert Fulton and his partner Robert Livingston procured the monopoly rights to the lower Mississippi River. In the autumn of 1811 their steamboat *New Orleans* made the first successful

voyage from Pittsburgh to New Orleans. Freight and passengers now could be carried upriver almost as easily as down—and at far less cost than by road. But the average lifespan of a river steamboat was only four to five years. Many were poorly constructed and maintained, many more were sunk by snags and other obstructions in the river, and some had their huge boilers explode.

In 1814, 20 steamboats pulled up to the docks at New Orleans; within 20 years their number had climbed to nearly 1,200. They mostly carried passengers, cotton, and sugar. By 1830 they ruled the waves on navigable western waters.

Steam opened the hinterlands to world trade, hauling barreled meats from Cincinnati, iron and coal from Pittsburgh, and cotton from Tennessee and Arkansas. Boats chugged up the Missouri River, helping to settle the country and to transport hides, timber, and grain to market. By 1860 stern-wheelers steamed the 2,200 miles up the Missouri River to Fort Benton, Montana.

ABOVE: *Stacked cotton bales leave little room for crewmen on the steamship* William Carig, *docked on the Mississippi River near Baton Rouge, Louisiana.*

OPPOSITE: *To assure every planter river frontage and give them easier access to the steamships, plantations were laid out in narrow strips, as shown on an 1858 map of the lower Mississippi River.*

The INDUSTRIAL REVOLUTION

American Ingenuity

If thou wilt come and do it, thou shalt have . . . the credit as well as the advantage of perfecting the first water-mill in America," wrote retired Quaker merchant Moses Brown. He was soliciting the help of Samuel Slater, who had apprenticed under the Arkwright system of water-powered cotton spinning in England. Slater passed outbound through British customs in 1789 with precise knowledge of the system. He carried no plans, as their export was illegal.

Thus did industry begin in the U.S., with bootleg technology based on the illegal transfer of trade secrets. Slater later immigrated to Rhode Island and, in 1793, built America's first successful mill in Pawtucket. To attract workers, he also built housing for the laborers' families, forming a village around the mill. Early manufacturing communities were often built in rural settings and were utopias when compared with the choked and grimy warrens of Britain's factories.

"I well recollect the state of admiration and satisfaction with which we sat by the hour, watching the beautiful movement of this new and wonderful machine," wrote Boston merchant Nathan Appleton of his 1814 meeting with inventor Francis Lowell. The mechanized loom was not a new invention—Lowell had studied looms in English factories before creating his own design. Crafted mostly of wood and powered by water, Lowell's rhythmic power loom soon had New England workers weaving cloth for the country's rapidly growing population.

Young women worked in the early factories, where they were housed. Late in her life, Harriet Robinson remembered her experiences as a mill worker from 1832 to 1848 in Lowell, Massachusetts. They were paid two dollars a week and were expected to put in nearly 14 hours a day. Most of the girls were between 16 and 25 and worked from eight to ten months a year; some taught school during the summer months. "The most prevailing incentive to labor was to secure the means of education for some male member of the family . . . to give him a college education . . . I have known more than one to give every cent of her wages, month after month, to her brother, that he might get the education necessary to enter some profession."

The textile business would grow and flourish in New England, thanks to its plentiful rivers and advances in technology. In early textile mills, the weight of water flowing into buckets turned the water wheels. Gears on their perimeters meshed with smaller pinion gears to drive the main drum, transmitting power to horizontal main shafts on alternate floors. These in turn drove overhead shafts whose belts also reached up through the ceiling. Shaft speed increased as drum sizes grew smaller. Belts from these shafts drove carding machines on the first floor, spinning frames on the second, looms on the third, and dressers on the fourth. Even after electric power became available, some Lowell mills were still using this system as late as the 1920s.

NORTH AND HALL

In 1813 a Connecticut armorer, Simeon North, did what Eli Whitney took public credit for but failed to do: produce guns with interchangeable parts. The first hundred or so of North's horse pistols were completely interchangeable and thus capable of quick repair on the battlefield. The government, however, added new demands to the specifications. Production slipped and quality suffered.

North's advances inspired others, including John H. Hall, manufacturer of a breechloading rifle at an armory in Harpers Ferry, Virginia. The U.S. Army in 1828 ordered 5,000 of the weapons. Hall used precision machines, files, gauges, and hard-nosed inspectors to create a process later adopted for mass-producing sewing machines, watches, and bicycles—the so-called "American system." But workers disliked the new rules; at Harpers Ferry a superintendent was shot for enforcing them. ■

Between 1820 and 1850 manufacturing was the fastest growing segment of the economy. With the canals, roads, and regional railroads extending navigable rivers into a transportation system, factories spread out to forge new products. Technical advances changed other industries as well; interchangeable parts spurred the manufacture of firearms and clocks and, later, agricultural tools, sewing machines, and other consumer goods. Factories replaced small shops and handicraft industries. Carpet weaving was a hand industry before 1845, but by 1860 it was being done largely on power looms. Blast furnaces and rolling mills sprang up. Coal replaced charcoal in smelt, and all over America smokestacks rose over industrial cities. As industrial processes changed, so too did the products they manufactured. By 1820 processors had learned how to preserve seafood. After 1840 vegetables and fruits could be canned and sold.

OPPOSITE: *Young doffers wait to "doff," or remove, full bobbins from spinning frames. These young boys worked in the Elk Cotton Mills of Fayetteville, Tennessee, in 1910.*

WESTWARD EXPANSION

The Spread of the Settlers

Fur trappers were among the first to see much of the West. By the early 1820s they were ranging the Plains and Rockies for beaver and trading at company posts along major rivers. In 1825 entrepreneur William Ashley and trapper Andrew Henry introduced the summer trading rendezvous in the mountains, a system of trade that quickly caught on. Other mountain men, including Kit Carson and Joseph Walker, began breaking trails.

In 1826 fur trapper and trader Jedediah Smith led an expedition southwest from the Great Salt Lake to the Pacific Ocean—the first such passage to California. He wrote: "In taking the charge of our Southwestern Expedition I followed the bent of my strong inclination to visit this unexplored country and unfold those hidden resources of wealth and bring to light those wonders which I readily imagined a country so extensive might contain. . . . I wanted to be the first to view a country on which the eyes of a white man had never gazed and to follow the course of rivers that run through a new land."

By 1840 trappers, their quarry scarce and their markets drying up, were concentrated in central Colorado. Their new calling was guiding settlers along the old trails. Since 1785 land surveyors had advanced the frontier, measuring out plots for the nation to grow into. Their legacy: a grid of survey lines that divides the nation neatly into one-square-mile chunks.

After 150 years of colonialism, only a few thousand souls had ventured west of the Appalachians. But after fewer than 80 years of U.S. independence 100,000 settlers had come to California, and the continent had been spanned.

The migration was facilitated by generous government land policies wedded to the survey system. In 1794, the governor of Spanish Louisiana had warned of a "new and vigorous people" to the east whose "method of spreading themselves and their policy are so much to be feared by Spain as are their arms." After the Louisiana Purchase in 1803, American emigration would go on to overwhelm Mexican military garrisons in both Texas and California, British claim to much of the Oregon Country, and the immemorial domain of the Indians.

Morris Birkbeck came from England in 1817 to settle in Illinois, and was impressed by the large number of emigrants moving toward Pittsburgh, jumping-off place for the frontier. "We have now fairly turned our backs on the old world, and find ourselves in the very stream of emigration. Old America seems to be breaking up, and moving westward. We are seldom out of sight, as we travel on this grand track towards the Ohio, of family groups. . . ."

Many wagon trains were outfitted in Independence, Missouri. The Santa Fe Trail, pioneered in 1822, took pioneers to New Mexico. It was the first major wagon road to the Far West. By 1843 Independence was the starting point of the Great Migration: wagons loaded with emigrants who were heading for Oregon Country. Many thought their chances of making it poor. In New York City Horace Greeley wrote, "This migration of more than a thousand persons in one body to Oregon wears an aspect of insanity."

Oregon lay 2,000 miles away. Getting there might take six months. "Travel, travel, TRAVEL," Dr. Marcus Whitman told the emigrants.

JAMES FENIMORE COOPER

An unlikely novelist, Cooper began writing suddenly and without premeditation. One evening he casually remarked to his wife that even he could write a better book than the English novel he had been reading. She immediately challenged him to do so. His first book, a novel of manners, was *Precaution*, published in 1820 when he was 31 years old. Within a year he had written *The Spy*, which was a huge success. In 1822 he moved to New York and completed more than 30 novels in quick succession. His fame quickly grew and spread worldwide.

But Mark Twain was not impressed. "Cooper's art has some defects," he wrote. "In one place in *Deerslayer*, and in the restricted space of two-thirds of a page, Cooper has scored 114 offenses against literary art out of a possible 115. It breaks the record."

Franz Schubert was a huge fan. In 1828 he pleaded from his deathbed for another Cooper novel to read while he lay dying. "I have read [his] *Last of the Mohicans*, *The Spy*, *The Pilot*, and *The Pioneers*," he wrote a friend. "If by any chance you have anything else of his, do please leave it for me. . . ." But within a week he was dead. ∎

"Nothing else will take you to the end of your journey . . . nothing is good for you that causes a moment's delay."

Land, gold, religious refuge—these had brought Europeans to the New World, and they lured Americans west. Within the decade Oregon-bound farmers traveled with boisterous forty-niners and devout Mormons. Indian attacks claimed lives, accidents claimed more, cholera more still. An average of ten graves would line each mile of the Oregon Trail by 1859.

A northern editor named John O'Sullivan was one of many Americans who saw the nation stretching from sea to sea, a country that would "overspread the continent allotted by Providence for the free development of our yearly multiplying millions." He called it the nation's Manifest Destiny. It became a catchphrase that gave license to further westward expansion.

ABOVE: *Weary from trekking westward, women and children rest near Colorado Springs. Some of the wagon trains were three miles long.*

NEXT: *A rainbow arches over this scenic view of western Nebraska that falls along the historic Oregon Trail.*

The TRAIL of TEARS

Displacing American Natives

Of all the sufferings and betrayals visited upon Native Americans, few are more wrenching than that of the Cherokees, Iroquoian Indians who lived in the mountains of eastern Tennessee and the western Carolinas and Georgia. Their population in 1650 was an estimated 22,500; they were spread over 40,000 square miles of the Appalachians. They modeled their government on that of the United States.

Under their chief, Junaluska, they fought alongside the whites against the Creek. Their farms, textiles, and houses were patterned after those of their white neighbors. One of their chiefs,

---

SEQUOYAH

The Cherokee scholar Sequoyah was born of a British trader named Nathaniel Gist and a Cherokee mother in the Tennessee country sometime between 1760 and 1770. He never learned to speak, read, or write English but was an accomplished silversmith, painter, and warrior. He served with the U.S. Army in the Creek War in 1813-14.

As an adult he became convinced that the secret of the white people's superior power was their written language. It enabled the whites to accumulate and transmit more knowledge than was possible for a people dependent on memory and word-of-mouth. Around 1809, helped by his daughter, he began working to develop a system of writing for the Cherokees. He experimented with pictographs and with symbols that represented the syllables of spoken Cherokee. By 1821 he had a syllabary of 86 symbols that represented all the syllables of the Cherokee language. It was a simple system that soon spread throughout the Cherokee nation and resulted in books and newspapers in Cherokee and schoolchildren studying their language in written form in their schools. Yet Sequoyah's great accomplishment would not be enough to save his people. ∎

Sequoyah, invented a system for writing Cherokee. They soon had a written constitution and a Cherokee Bible. But when gold was discovered in the hills of Georgia, it brought a tidal wave of white intruders that demanded the land.

The Cherokee Legislative Council issued a statement in July 1830: "Inclination to remove from this land has no abiding place in our hearts, and when we move we shall move by the course of nature to sleep under this ground which the Great Spirit gave to our ancestors and which now covers them in their undisturbed peace."

But a small group of Cherokee, motivated perhaps by greed, in December 1835, acquiesced. The Treaty of New Echota ceded all of their lands east of the Mississippi to the state of Georgia for five million dollars. Most of the Indians hated the treaty and vowed to fight it. They managed to get their case before the U.S. Supreme Court, then under Chief Justice John Marshall. The Court sided with the Indians, ruling that the state had no jurisdiction over the Cherokee and no valid claim to their lands.

But President Andrew Jackson was determined that the Cherokee lands would pass into the hands of the whites. "John Marshall has made his decision," he said, "now let him enforce it." Of course Marshall couldn't, and under the Indian Removal Act of 1830, the Cherokee were ordered transported to Indian Territory in the West.

The Army began rounding them up and housing them in 30 temporary stockades in North Carolina, Georgia, Alabama, and Tennessee. From there they were moved to 11 internment camps, mostly in Tennessee. By the end of July 1838 some 15,000 Cherokee, virtually all of the tribe in the East, were imprisoned in the camps. Seven camps in and around Charleston, Tennessee, alone held nearly 5,000 Indians.

A few escaped. The Oconaluftee Cherokee produced an 1819 treaty that made them American citizens on lands that did not belong to the Cherokee Nation. They refused to join the roundup, and North Carolina ultimately recognized their rights. Other bands simply took to the hills as the roundup began, hiding out in the thickets and hollows of the Great Smoky Mountains. They eventually joined up with the Oconaluftee Band to become the Eastern Band of the Cherokees, and they live today in the hills and valleys surrounding Great Smoky Mountains National Park.

During the fall and winter of 1838 and 1839 the eviction of the Cherokee began. Three detachments made up of 2,800 Indians were put aboard boats and made the journey west by river. Most traveled overland on existing roads in groups of 700 to 1,600. The movement was badly organized. Food ran short and winter arrived. The food they did manage to find was often of poor quality. Draft animals hauled possessions but had to forage for their feed; drought reduced the available supply. The people walked alongside their animals, carrying what they could. It was a forced march and came to be called the Trail of Tears. More than 4,000 Indians died en route.

An Army private named John G. Burnett wrote, "I saw the helpless Cherokees arrested and dragged from their homes, and driven at the bayonet point into the stockades. And in the chill of a drizzling rain on an October morning I saw them loaded like cattle or sheep into six hundred and forty-five wagons and started toward the west . . . the sufferings of the Cherokees were awful . . . And I have known as many as twenty-two of them to die in one night of pneumonia due to ill treatment, cold and exposure."

One historian lamented, "The Cherokee are probably the most tragic instance of what could have succeeded in American Indian policy and didn't. . . they may be Christian, they may be literate, they may have a government like ours, but ultimately they are Indian. And in the end, being Indian is what kills them."

ABOVE: *Members of the Cherokee tribe undertake a midwinter trek to Indian Territory, later called Oklahoma. More than 4,000 died along the way.*

TEXAS REVOLUTION

Fighting for Land

In 1821 Mexico gained independence from Spain and began to welcome settlers from America into its Texas region, but as more and more came, some illegally bringing their slaves with them, Mexico began to limit immigration. Colonists began lobbying to govern themselves.

One of the Texas settlers, Stephen F. Austin, had received a grant of 200,000 acres along the lower Brazos and Colorado Rivers. By 1834 he had induced 8,000 to 9,000 settlers to live there. Stephen Austin and other aggrieved colonists set out to Mexico City to have their grievances addressed. They expected a friendly hearing from Mexican President Antonio Lopez de Santa Anna,

---

STEPHEN AUSTIN

Raised on the Missouri frontier, Stephen Austin became founder in the 1820s of a major American colony in Texas.

When an economic panic in 1819 forced his father to give up his business in Missouri, Stephen followed him to Texas to attempt colonization. The father obtained a grant of land from the Mexican government but died. Stephen took up the effort. He became one of the major figures in the struggle between Mexico and the U.S. that culminated in war.

A strong proponent of slavery, he helped defeat an effort to ban it in Texas. He tried to persuade the Mexican government to give the Texas region special status so American settlers could enjoy self-government. He was charged with having treasonable tendencies and imprisoned by Mexico when this effort failed.

In 1836 Sam Houston defeated him for the presidency of the new Republic of Texas.

He has the distinction of being born in one town named for his family—Austinville, Virginia, November 3, 1793—and dying in another—Austin, Texas, December 27, 1836. ∎

---

but were instead imprisoned in Mexico City and charged with encouraging insurrection. When released in 1835, Austin returned home and found that fighting between the colonists and Mexican troops had already begun. Santa Anna, he heard, was sending reinforcements.

The Texans declared independence at the village of Washington-on-Brazos in March 1836. They wrote a constitution that declared slavery in Texas lawful. In April, commanded by Sam Houston, they defeated Santa Anna's army at the Battle of San Jacinto. The battle lasted just 20 minutes, and Houston fought much of it with a boot full of blood from a wound to his leg.

Texas petitioned for admittance to the Union, but neither President Andrew Jackson nor his successor, Martin Van Buren, was eager to accept it. Mexico naturally did not recognize Texas as an independent nation, so admitting it into the Union might very well lead to further conflict with Mexico. The Democratic presidential candidate in 1844, James K. Polk of Tennessee, ran for office promising "all of Texas, and all of Oregon." When Polk won, it made war with Mexico nearly a certainty; a victory would give the U.S. not only Texas but also California, a rich territory with valuable coastal ports.

In the spring of 1846 Mexican troops clashed with U.S. cavalry patrols on the northern bank of the Rio Grande River, and Polk had the excuse he needed for a war. The American invasion of Mexico took place in 1846 and 1847, and the result was a total defeat for Mexico. On September 13, 1847, the last major battle of the war was fought on the heights of Chapultepec.

In February 1848 the U.S. imposed a treaty of peace at the town of Guadeloupe Hidalgo. Mexico surrendered Texas, New Mexico, and California—an enormous area that stretched

from the Gulf of Mexico to the Pacific Ocean. Yet many northerners feared slaveholders would take their slaves into this valuable territory, further troubling the uneasy peace between North and South.

ABOVE: *Sam Houston migrated to Texas while it was still under Mexican rule. After Texans wrote their Declaration of Independence, he enthusiastically served as president of Texas from 1836–1838.*

REMEMBERING
the ALAMO

A Battle of Legend

A quiet 18th-century Franciscan mission in San Antonio, Texas, founded to bring education and Christianity to the local Indians, gained lasting fame as the site of a historic battle. It pitched a small group of determined fighters for the independence of Texas against the forces of Mexico. Its participants became legendary as stalwart defenders of a lost cause; the suspense of its outcome caught the attention of the whole country.

The mission itself was founded in 1718 by Franciscans. By the end of the 18th century, however, it was abandoned. Now and then, after 1801, its chapel was occupied by Spanish troops, who named the place Alamo, Spanish for "cottonwood." A grove of the trees stood nearby.

In December 1835 a band of Texans attacked Mexican troops stationed there, forced them out of the city, and took up residence at the Alamo. Two months later, the Mexican army of Santa Anna arrived. The Texans were caught by surprise but prepared to defend themselves and the Alamo.

To Texans today, Antonio Lopez de Santa Anna is perhaps the chief villain of their state's

history. He was born in Mexico on February 21, 1794, and by 1833 he had been democratically elected president of Mexico. But he thought Mexico not quite ready for democracy, so pronounced himself dictator. His army of somewhere between 2,000 and 6,000 men surrounded the Alamo in February 1836.

Among the defenders were famous names that reverberate today. Davy Crockett and Colonel James "Jim" Bowie, of Bowie knife fame, were there. Bowie had been born in Georgia in 1796 but had come to Texas in search of silver and gold. He made friends of the Tejanos, unusual for his time, and was in command of a group of Texas volunteers in San Antonio when William Travis arrived. Travis was leading regular army troops, and he and Bowie shared an uneasy command during much of the siege. But at the time of the attack, Bowie was evidently confined to his cot, laid low by a lung infection.

FROM THE ALAMO, FEBRUARY 24, 1836

To the People of Texas & All Americans in the World: Fellow Citizens & Compatriots—I am besieged, by a thousand or more of the Mexicans under Santa Anna—I have sustained a continual Bombardment & cannonade for 24 hours & have not lost a man.—The enemy has demanded a surrender at discretion, otherwise the garrison are to be put to the sword, if the fort is taken…I shall never surrender nor retreat. Then, I call on you in the name of Liberty, of patriotism & every thing dear to the American character, to come to our aid, with all dispatch—The enemy is receiving reinforcements daily & will no doubt increase to three or four thousand in four or five days. If this call is neglected, I am determined to sustain myself as long as possible & die like a soldier who never forgets what is due to his own honor & that of his country—Victory or Death. The Lord is on our side.

–William Barret Travis
Col. Comdt. P.S.

Davy Crockett was born in Tennessee on August 17, 1786. He served as a scout for a militia in 1813, and in 1815 he explored Alabama, looking for a suitable spot to settle. In 1835, accompanied by several companions, he set out for Texas, expecting "to explore the Texes well before I return." He was impressed with the territory. He wrote home, "I must say as to what I have seen of Texas it is the garden spot of the world. The best land and the best prospects for health I ever saw." As a member of the Texas volunteers, he found himself at the Alamo in February 1836.

The defenders of the Alamo numbered perhaps as few as 184 men. They resisted the Mexican siege for 13 days, but on the morning of March 6 the Mexicans stormed through a breach in the outer courtyard wall and overwhelmed them. All but a few of the defenders were put to death. There is no accurate count of Mexican casualties, but historians estimate them at between 600 and 1,600. The loss of the Alamo roused the Texans, who defeated the Mexicans at the Battle of San Jacinto on April 21, capturing Santa Anna himself.

The Mexican army maintained control of the garrison. They pulled down some of the outer walls, including one called Crockett's Palisade, making it difficult for the Americans to refortify it. When Texas forces entered San Antonio on June 4, 1836, they found just 18 Mexican soldiers holding the fort. Both sides acted peaceably and withdrew, the Mexicans on June 6 and the Texans a few weeks later. In 1905 the state of Texas had acquired title to the mission. Today it has been restored and is maintained as a historic site.

OPPOSITE: *Bright blue skies shine over the chapel at the Alamo. The original mission was founded by Franciscan monks in 1718.*

NEXT: *Davy Crockett raises his rifle over his head as he leads the Texan defenders of the Alamo against the Mexican soldiers within the walls of the fortress.*

PARCELING OUT the LAND

First Steps to Freedom

Since the War of 1812, western lands had been much sought after, and the land-office business had boomed. Land revenues poured into the Treasury, only to return west to finance canals, roads, and additional land surveys. But in 1833 President Andrew Jackson reported a skewed balance of payments: The 38 million dollars received from land sales since 1789 did not equal the 49 million invested in western lands.

Settlers and speculators had operated in uneasy partnership since the earliest days of the frontier. Settlers wanted land; speculators wanted money. When land sales were booming, it seemed that everyone was a speculator. "I never saw a busier place than Chicago," wrote a woman visiting from England in 1836. "As the gentlemen of our party walked the streets, store-keepers hailed them from their doors, with offers of farms, and all manner of land-lots, advising them to speculate before the price of land rose higher."

The "fever for speculation" was periodically broken by financial panics that kept the land market chaotic throughout the 19th century. Unsound currency touched off depressions in 1819 and 1837. During the late 1850s deadlocks over railroad locations stemmed western growth as the country slid into civil war. Later, beginning in the 1880s, free homesteads, European investment, and massive land grants to railroads and states all propelled a series of land booms.

The depression of 1837 soured speculation, as prices plummeted. A hundred midwestern towns never made it off their grandly inscribed rectangular plats.

Another major blow to speculation was the Pre-emption Act of 1841. Previously, first settlers—or "squatters"—on public lands could purchase the property if they had improved it. But they could never acquire a secure title to the land. When it was surveyed and put up for auction, speculators could buy it out from under them. With little money and no title, squatters led a precarious existence. They were even in danger from claim jumpers who might resort to force to evict a family of squatters.

They urged their congressmen to pass legislation that would allow them to get title to their land without having to bid for it at an auction. Temporary preemption laws in the 1830s helped somewhat but angered Eastern businessmen, who feared their cheap labor would move west if land was too easy to acquire.

Henry Clay in 1841 devised a compromise: an act to provide squatters the right to buy 160 acres of surveyed public land at a minimum price of $1.25 per acre before the land was sold at auction. The act remained in effect for 50 years but led to enormous corruption as nonsettlers acquired great tracts of land illegally. Its failure led in part to passage of the Homestead Act of 1862, which, by giving squatters a legal system for acquiring their 160 acres of land, in effect legalized preemption.

Homesteading failed in its attempt to settle the Great Plains. The act offered 160 acres free to anyone who wanted it, and optimistic "sod-busters," as the farmers were called because of the sod houses they built, eagerly took up the challenge. They used three-foot-long strips of topsoil like bricks to construct their homes, which stayed cool in summer and warm in winter but were messy when it rained. And all the creatures of the

soil—worms, bugs, snakes, and mice—lived in the ceiling and walls.

Officials doubted the region could be successfully cultivated, though Mormons had proved otherwise even farther west. The Army's commanding officer on the plains, Gen. William Tecumseh Sherman, reported that the land west of Iowa was "fit only for Nomadic tribes of Indians, Tartars, or Buffaloes."

Settlers came anyway. A report in an eastern newspaper described Kansas as an ocean of "luxuriant grass and flowers. Day after day a man may travel, and still one word will characterize all he sees—Beautiful!" By 1900, more than 80 million acres had been claimed by 600,000 homestead farmers. By 1910 many states had doubled the size of a homestead to 320 acres; Nebraska allowed 640.

One item the homesteaders brought with them—barbed wire—led to conflict with cattle ranchers. Invented in 1874, it kept cattle from straying vast distances and enabled separation of choice herds to assist in selective breeding programs. But it also brought homesteaders swarming onto the plains—and allowed them to fence off pastures and water holes the cattlemen regarded as rightfully theirs. Such conflicts led to years of bitterness and bloodshed across the plains.

ABOVE: *A new home rises on the plains in the Oklahoma Territory; two million acres of former Indian Territory were opened to settlement on April 22, 1889. For some families, an Oklahoma homestead was their first chance to own property.*

FROM *A LOST LADY*

The Old West had been settled by dreamers, great-hearted adventurers who were unpractical to the point of magnificence; a courteous brotherhood strong in attack but weak in defense, who would conquer but not hold. Now all the vast territory they had won was to be at the mercy of men like Ivy Peters who had never dared anything, never risked anything. They would drink up the mirage, dispel the morning freshness, root out the great brooding spirit of freedom, the generous, easy life of the great landholders. The space, the colour, the princely carelessness of the pioneer they would destroy and cut up into profitable bits, as the match factory splinters up the primeval forest. All the way from the Missouri to the mountains this generation of shrewd young men, trained to petty economies by hard times, would do exactly what Ivy Peters had done when he drained the Forrester marsh.

–Willa Cather

MANIFEST DESTINY

A Call for the Land

The belief that gave the United States theoretical license to expand its empire from the Atlantic Ocean to the Pacific—and even beyond, to Alaska, Hawaii, and the Philippines—was called Manifest Destiny. Journalist John L. O'Sullivan coined the phrase in his *United States Magazine and Democratic Review* in the issue of July 1845. He prophesied "the fulfillment of our manifest destiny to overspread the continent allotted by Providence . . ." When Congress took up the issue of westward expansion, three specific areas concerned them: the Mexican-American War, the question of the Oregon Territory (claimed both by the U.S. and England) and the annexation of the huge Texas territory.

Several forces in the U.S. coincided to encourage the concept of Manifest Destiny. A high birth rate coupled with increased immigration was contributing to a growing population. As most families were farmers, the more children they had, the more labor they had to plant, sow, and harvest—so a large family was a plus to a farmer. Between 1800 and 1850, the U.S. population increased from more than 5 million to more than 23 million. The new Americans needed land, and new territories were beckoning them.

Also, an economic depression in 1818 and another in 1837 tended to move people toward the frontier, where they could acquire land that was cheap, or, in some cases, even free. To own land was highly desirable: It hinted at wealth, political power, and self-sufficiency. And last, merchants looked hungrily at the long western coast where new ports could be built and a new marketplace could arise to import and export more goods.

To people in favor of expansion, the issue was clear: To prosper and grow, the country had to enlarge. They invoked Thomas Jefferson's views, that yeoman farmers were the backbone of the country. Then, too, some Americans worried that Great Britain had her eyes on the Pacific Coast and bore watching.

At least two peoples were not as enthusiastic about Manifest Destiny: the Mexicans and the American Indians. Both of these groups stood in the way of the United States' desire for more land, and both lost many lives in trying to hold onto their lands.

INAUGURAL ADDRESS
MARCH 4, 1845

In the earlier stages of our national existence the opinion prevailed with some that our system of confederated States could not operate successfully over an extended territory, and serious objections have at different times been made to the enlargement of our boundaries. These objections were earnestly urged when we acquired Louisiana. Experience has shown that they were not well founded. The title of numerous Indian tribes to vast tracts of country has been extinguished; new States have been admitted into the Union . . . As our boundaries have been enlarged and our agricultural population has been spread over a large surface, our federative system has acquired additional strength and security . . . It is confidently believed that our system may be safely extended to the utmost bounds of our territorial limits, and that as it shall be extended the bonds of our Union, so far from being weakened, will become stronger.

—President James Knox Polk

Mexican historian Miguel Angel González Quiroga has said that Manifest Destiny "has an immense fascination for many of us in Mexico . . . It is dangerous to underestimate the power of an idea. Especially one which captures the imagination of a people. Manifest Destiny was such an idea. To extend American democracy to the rest of the continent was to place a mantle of legitimacy on what was essentially an insatiable ambition for land." Quiroga concludes, "Manifest Destiny was a graceful way to justify something unjustifiable."

The Indians, considered by most Americans of the time as an inferior people who would never fit into the life of the East, were unceremoniously shifted to regions beyond the frontier where they could maintain their "uncivilized" ways. Some saw the hypocrisy in this: Many of the Indians who were removed were as sophisticated as whites. The literacy rate of the Cherokee Nation was higher than that of the white South up through the Civil War. Yet Manifest Destiny insisted they be moved out of the way of America's expansion. Texas, the enormous and thinly populated region of Mexico, was irresistible to the expansionists, not least because it held the future California.

"Broadly stated," American historian David M. Pletcher at Indiana University has said, "Manifest Destiny was a conviction that God intended North America to be under the control of Americans. It's a kind of early projection of Anglo-Saxon supremacy, and there was a racist element to it. But there was also an idealistic element. It is very hard to measure the two. If you asked a person to define Manifest Destiny, he might tell you it is an ideal, or he might say, 'Well, we want the land and this is the easiest way to justify our taking it.'"

OPPOSITE: *The spirit of Manifest Destiny floats westward in an 1873 painting by John Gast. She carries a schoolbook in one arm and strings telegraph wire behind her with the other. On the ground below, Native Americans and bison retreat before her, and the signs of western expansion—trains, ships, covered wagons, and settlers—follow.*

The RUSH for GOLD

Miners and Boomtowns

The fabled California gold rush began on January 24, 1848. A carpenter named James Marshall and his crew were constructing a water-powered sawmill on the American River for trader John Sutter. Marshall saw a glittering at the bottom of the waterway. "I reached my hand down and picked it up; it made my heart thump, for I was certain it was gold. The piece was about the size and shape of a pea. Then I saw another." The rush for gold had begun.

In Washington, President James Polk confirmed the news from California. "The accounts of the abundance of gold in that territory are of such extraordinary character as would scarcely command belief were they not corroborated by authentic reports of officers in the public service."

Gold seekers—who came to be called Forty-Niners—made their way to California by any means possible. Some made the long trek overland, but those with money bought tickets on steamships or clipper ships. From the East Coast, the ships would sail all the way down the coast of South America, round Cape Horn, and put the potential prospectors ashore in San Francisco. The journey required at least three months at sea.

A San Franciscan named Sam Brannan was first to recognize where the real money was to be made. He quickly bought up the variety of tools the gold seekers would need—pickaxes, pans, shovels—then hawked them through the streets. "Gold!" he would shout. "Gold on the American River." A metal pan he had bought for twenty cents a few days earlier he was now willing to part with for fifteen dollars. In nine weeks he made $36,000.

By the end of 1849 as many as 80,000 had left friends, families, and fields to pan for California gold. Some mining towns survived the boom; most did not. "In no other land . . . have towns so absolutely died and disappeared," Mark Twain observed in 1871.

It was a freewheeling world with little or no government, no military, no taxes to be paid or tax collectors to collect them, no judicial system. To extract the tiny flakes from streams, prospectors swirled pans of silt or shoveled dirt into strainers. "I tell you this mining among the mountains is a dog's life," one wrote home. A few of the early miners struck it rich, but the days when fortunes could be obtained by simply bending down and picking them up quickly passed.

Towns with colorful names sprang up: Hangtown, Gouge Eye, Rough and Ready, Whiskeytown. It was largely a classless society, and even women could profit. Many were prostitutes, but others ran boarding houses, cooked, did laundry for the miners. By mid-1849, the quick and easy gold had all been mined, but the Forty-Niners still arrived in droves.

To clothe them, Levi Strauss began manufacturing heavy canvas trousers, which the miners liked. New York butcher Philip Armour walked all the way to California, where he opened a meat

market in Placerville. With the money he made he built a meat processing plant in Milwaukee. John Studebaker, also in Placerville, sold wheelbarrows; he took his profits home to Indiana and created the family's wagon-making business. Henry Wells and William Fargo offered a badly needed service: secure and honest banking, transportation, even delivery of the mail.

San Francisco boomed. In the 1840s only a few hundred people lived there, but it was soon building 30 new houses a day. It also averaged two murders a day. In 18 months a parcel of land that cost $16 in 1847 was going for $45,000. In less than two years, the city burned to the ground six times. In the 1850s perhaps half a billion dollars' worth of gold passed through the city. Soon it had its own opera, theaters, and more newspapers than any city except London.

Foreigners as well as Americans became Forty-Niners. A Norwegian in the gold fields wrote home: "Fine order and peace prevail here . . . [since] an insult will usually be paid back with a piece of lead." Chinese, Chileans, Mexicans, Irish,

Germans, French, Turks—all came to join the gold rush. Most intended to get rich, then return home. The Chinese took the gold they found to San Francisco, where they melted it down into woks, frying pans, and other utensils, which they then carried home to China. To make a profit from the foreign miners, the California legislature passed the Foreign Miners Tax in 1850, which collected twenty dollars a month from every foreigner in the gold fields.

Mining companies brought in heavy ore-processing machinery, which replaced the shovel-and-pan prospectors. Many prospectors simply went home, but others pushed into Nevada and Colorado in the late 1850s, into Montana and Idaho in the '60s, and into the Black Hills of the Dakota Territory in the '70s.

ABOVE: *Miners work a sluice box in California ca 1850.*
OPPOSITE: *When panning for gold, ore is placed in a pan with water. The miner agitates the pan, allowing the gold particles to separate and settle in the bottom.*

1850
THROUGH
1899

A NATION COMES *of* AGE

LANDING ON THIS GREAT CONTINENT IS like going to sea," wrote Hector St. John de Crèvecoeur of a visit to America in 1782. By the mid-19th century, the waters of the sea were troubled, and the ship of state was being tossed by rising tempests.

Forces set in motion early in the country's history were about to meet at bloody battlefields across much of the new nation. Republican versus Democrat, slavery versus Free Labor, North versus South, manufacturer versus farmer, urbanization versus the rural life: All served to drive sections of the country apart.

It was also a period of movement and growth. Americans built railroads and newspapers, mined gold and petroleum, forged steel and factories, and dammed rivers. Homesteads and ranches carpeted the West; a flood tide of immigrants turned the wheels of northern industry. Workers made themselves heard through growing labor unions. Alexis de Tocqueville spotted a force that would flower in the next century: "If I were asked . . . to what the singular prosperity and growing strength of that people [the Americans] ought mainly to be attributed, I should reply: To the superiority of their women." By the end of the 19th century, the United States would resemble what Samuel Taylor Coleridge had written in 1833, "The possible destiny of the United States of America—as a nation of a hundred million of freemen—stretching from the Atlantic to the Pacific, living under the laws of Alfred, and speaking the language of Shakespeare and Milton, is an august conception."

Beyond the James River in 1865 stood the burned ruins of Richmond, Virginia, the former capital of the Confederacy.

The UNDERGROUND RAILROAD

Escape to Liberty

The secret routes and daring operators of the Underground Railroad helped thousands of slaves find freedom in the North and Canada. Benjamin Pearson built his house in Iowa with a trapdoor and a secret basement where he hid runaway slaves. Bold John Brown liberated slaves in Missouri and led them to Canada. Master of disguise John Fairfield posed 28 slaves as a funeral procession in Kentucky and marched them to freedom. Slave Henry "Box" Brown had himself shipped from Richmond to Philadelphia in a wooden crate. Jane Lewis, a black woman, regularly rowed fugitives across the Ohio River. Escaping on a stolen horse, Henry Bibb coolly passed as a free man all the way from Indian Territory to Canada. Nicknamed Moses, Harriet Tubman escaped to the North and then made many perilous trips back to the South to escort other slaves to freedom.

HARRIET BEECHER STOWE

So you're the little woman who wrote the book that made this great war," President Lincoln is reported to have said when he was introduced to Harriet Beecher Stowe. Her book, Uncle Tom's Cabin, was a heartrending story of the cruelty of slavery. First published during 1851–52 as a serial in an abolitionist newspaper, then in 1852 as a book, Uncle Tom's Cabin strengthened and spread antislavery sentiment among Northerners, already angered by the Fugitive Slave Act of 1850. More than 300,000 copies of the book were sold within a year. Southerners claimed that the book was not true to life. They called Mrs. Stowe a "vile wretch in petticoats." ■

Runaways usually braved the hazards of the South alone, walking and getting food from blacks along the way. In border and free states abolitionists sheltered fugitives, calling their network of way stations the Underground Railroad. Ingenuity supplied a few escape routes; runaways rode trains disguised as whites in mourning or hid in shipping crates.

As the system for helping slaves escape to the North from the South developed, some of the terms of railroading came to be used. Routes were lines, safe places to rest were stations, the men and women assisting along the way were conductors, the slaves themselves were often called freight or packages. Its branches extended throughout 14 of the northern states and into Canada, a country where slavery was forbidden and into which the fugitive-slave hunters could not pursue the fleeing slaves.

The Fugitive Slave Act of 1850, passed as part of a compromise to pacify Southerners, complicated matters. After its passage, escaped slaves who lived in free states could be seized and returned to the South. The legislation made it possible for a black person in the North, even one who had lived there 15 or 20 years, to be seized on the presentation of an affidavit of a Southern slaveholder. The fugitive could not testify or summon witnesses or have a jury trial. A federal commissioner would decide the slave's fate, and appeals were not possible. Federal marshals enforced the act. The marshals themselves could be fined a thousand dollars if they refused to apprehend a fugitive. Anyone concealing or helping a fugitive was subject to a similar fine, plus civil damages, plus a possible six months in jail.

Along intricate and shifting routes, northerners who hated slavery felt it their duty to help runaway slaves to the safety of Canada. Famous for her novel *Uncle Tom's Cabin*, Harriet Beecher Stowe was among them. She gathered information of fugitive slaves through her contact with the Underground Railroad in Cincinnati, Ohio.

Another abolitionist, the Reverend John Rankin, who lived in Ohio, helped many slaves. He was the prototype of the man who aided the fleeing Eliza and her baby in *Uncle Tom's Cabin*. Of the Underground Railroad, he said, "There was no secret society organized. There were no secret oaths taken, nor promises of secrecy extorted. And yet there were no betrayals."

Nicknamed "President of the Underground Railroad," Levi Coffin assisted more than 2,000 runaway slaves. He was born in 1789 on a North Carolina farm. He became a schoolteacher and in 1821 established a Sunday school where the region's slaves could come to learn Bible stories and Christian hymns. A devout Quaker, he hated slavery. In 1826, he moved north to Newport, Indiana—present-day Fountain City—where he discovered that he had accidentally stumbled upon one of the way stations of the Underground Railroad. Coffin and his wife Catherine devoted their lives—as well as much of the money Levi was acquiring as a successful merchant—to helping fugitives on their way. His home became a well-known depot, and his neighbors were called upon and persuaded to contribute food, clothing, and supplies for the runaways.

With the outbreak of the Civil War, Coffin devoted himself to helping the newly liberated slaves. He journeyed to England in 1864 to raise money for the freed slaves and to Paris in 1867 to attend, as a delegate, the International Anti-Slavery Conference. By the time of his death on September 16, 1877, in Cincinnati, Ohio, he had seen the end of slavery.

ABOVE: *Harriet Tubman, standing at far left, poses with fellow African Americans, some of them former slaves she helped flee along the Underground Railroad. She escaped from slavery to the North but returned to the South many times to assist other runaways.*

The PONY EXPRESS

Delivering the Mail

The famous advertisement—"Wanted. Young, skinny, wiry fellows. Not over 18. Must be expert riders. Willing to risk death daily. Orphans preferred"— called attention to an exciting new enterprise: the Pony Express. During its brief life it provided mail service between St. Joseph, Missouri, and Sacramento, California. Riders on horseback rode 1,800 miles back and forth and changed horses at 157 stations along the way. It took an average of 10 days for a rider to make the entire trip.

Some 400 horses, including Morgans, mustangs, pintos, and thoroughbreds, were bought for the riders. At least 183 men rode for the Pony Express; they were paid $100 a month. At first, it cost a customer $5 to send a half-ounce letter, but by the time the service ended, that price was down to $1.

The service caught the imagination of Americans—a flood of books and movies would follow—but it was a disastrous financial failure for its backers, who put up $700,000 and lost it all. The completion of the transcontinental telegraph system, on October 24, 1861, put a quick end to the Pony Express, which had operated only from April 3, 1860, to late October 1861.

In the early 1800s, the mail came by pouch, if at all. Postage was due on delivery and cost as much as 25 cents a sheet, so some correspondents wrote from top to bottom, turned the page 90 degrees, and wrote top to bottom again to minimize the number of pages in each letter. By 1800, mail delivery extended as far west as Indiana and Mississipppi, which were served by 903 post offices. By the mid-1800s the California gold rush extended the demand for mail to the Pacific Coast, first by clipper ship and steamer to San Francisco, later by overland stagecoach lines and the Pony Express.

Faster ways of sending messages began to emerge in the 1830s. Samuel F. B. Morse began developing a practical electromagnetic telegraph in 1832. In 1843, Congress awarded him a $30,000 grant to construct a line between the District of Columbia and Baltimore, the country's first. The rhythmic clicking of Morse code soon spread across the land. Newspapers were quick to use the "lightning line" and carried "flashes" about the Mexican War in 1846. Telegraph news columns and news agencies followed. The first transcontinental telegraph message was sent in 1861—word of California's loyalty to the Union. By 1866 nearly 100,000 miles of wire connected every sizable town, and the lightning line had become indispensable to government, commerce, and the press.

The spread of railroads throughout the nation greatly impacted mail delivery. The first mail to move by train came as early as 1832, on a route from Philadelphia to Lancaster, Pennsylvania. Railroads and telegraph lines, "Siamese twins of Commerce," followed the central route of the Pony Express. Telegraph companies won exclusive contracts along railroad rights-of-way and reciprocated by wiring messages to prevent accidents and to dispatch trains.

By 1869, railroads connected the coasts and soon moved most of the country's mail; by 1930 more than 10,000 trains were employed. Service to the countryside lagged, however, and farmers had to agitate until 1902 for rural free delivery, which laid the groundwork for the 1913 advent of parcel post.

For airlines carrying the U.S. mail in 1940, routes from California to New York were the highest in volume and profit. Although mail contracts initially provided the lifeblood for the fledgling airlines, by 1940 revenues from passengers were more than double those from mail.

Despite competition from the telegraph and eventually the telephone, mail volume continued to grow. In 1886, some 3.7 billion pieces of mail were processed; by 1985 the volume had climbed to 140 billion, the only interim dip coming in the Great Depression. Seventy-five post offices in 1790 became 76,945 in 1901, a steady rise except after the Civil War. In 1971 the Post Office Department—and generations of political patronage—gave way to the U.S. Postal Service, an independent federal agency.

FROM *ROUGHING IT*

In a little while all interest was taken up in . . . watching for the pony-rider—the fleet messenger who sped across the continent from St. Joe to Sacramento, carrying letters nineteen hundred miles in eight days. . . . The pony-rider was usually a little bit of a man, brimful of spirit and endurance. No matter what time of the day or night his watch came on, and no matter whether it was winter or summer, raining, snowing, hailing, or sleeting . . . he must be always ready to leap into the saddle and be off like the wind! He rode fifty miles without stopping, by daylight, moonlight, starlight, or through the blackness of darkness. . . . He rode a splendid horse that was born for a racer and fed and lodged like a gentleman; kept him at his utmost speed for ten miles, and then, as he came crashing up to the station where stood two men holding fast a fresh, impatient steed, the transfer of rider and mailbag was made in the twinkling of an eye. . . . There were about eighty pony-riders in the saddle all the time, night and day, stretching in a long, scattering procession from Missouri to California.

—Mark Twain

OPPOSITE: *Pony Express riders stop to get fresh horses in this painting by Frederic Remington.*

The CIVIL WAR

The Failure of Compromise

Congress attempted to resolve the impasse over slavery's place in new states and acquired territories through the Compromise of 1850. Southern leaders, who had opposed admitting California as a free state, acquiesced in exchange for passage of the Fugitive Slave Act. But, compromise or no, the heart of the dispute remained. The South needed more slave states to keep pace with the North in Senate representation. Northern abolitionists demanded immediate freedom for slaves. Southern fire-eaters threatened immediate secession from the Union.

Slaveholders were intent on spreading slavery everywhere, a notion made more threatening to the North when the Supreme Court ruled in the 1857 Dred Scott case that Congress could not forbid slavery in any territory and that African Americans could never be citizens.

Illinois attorney Abraham Lincoln captured the presidency with a promise to contain slavery. To the South the worst had happened. Its enemies were united; the President-elect was a puppet of the North. The South sensed its choices narrow to two: face the eventual abolition of slavery, or leave the Union. In December 1860 South Carolina answered, "We secede."

"In all history," said William Tecumseh Sherman to a southern friend in 1860, "no nation of mere agriculturists ever made successful war against a nation of mechanics. . . . You are bound to fail." Few in the South imagined failure in the spring of 1861. What did it matter that the North had more factories and more men? Confederate soldiers felt that they could beat back the Yankees, no matter how many there were.

The Confederate president, Jefferson Davis, knew that valor alone would not defeat the North. He commenced building a war economy from the ground up. When men ran short, the Confederacy conscripted them. States' rights would have to take a backseat if the South was to win the war.

Lt. General Winfield Scott wanted to bring the North's considerable resources to bear on the South. In 1860 the North had 110,000 manufacturing establishments; the South had 18,000. The North had 21,973 miles of railroad and 451 locomotives; the south had 9,283 miles serviced by just 19 locomotives. Scott advised: Blockade the South's ports; split it along the Mississippi. Blows to the Confederate States' commerce and communications would "bring them to terms with less bloodshed than any other plan." The public scorned Scott's Anaconda Plan. It wanted battles won, fast. "Forward to Richmond!" it cried, and an ill-prepared Army of the Potomac marched to its first defeat at Bull Run.

The North fixed early on capturing the Confederate capital: Richmond, Virginia. After Bull Run in 1861 the Union forces returned in 1862 and were driven to retreat by Robert E. Lee's Army of Northern Virginia in the Seven Days' Battle. That autumn found the Army of the Potomac back across its namesake river.

General Lee was not satisfied. His victories in Virginia had won little more than time. Defeating the Union Army on Union soil, however, might win the war. At least, some southern leaders hoped, it would bring European recognition of the Confederacy, giving it legitimacy on the world

stage. However, Lee's northward thrust into Maryland was stymied at the Battle of Antietam.

Abraham Lincoln also had his eye on Europe. The Emancipation Proclamation, issued on January 1, 1863, gave the rebelling states the choice of returning to the Union or having their slaves declared free. Rejected by the South,

Lincoln's terms had their intended effect. Opposed to slavery and dubious of Confederate success, France and Britain remained neutral.

The Army of the Potomac made Lincoln's proclamation ring hollow. It tried a third time for Richmond and again was pummeled by Lee; another attempt was turned back by nothing more than bad weather. A New Yorker mailed home discontent: "I am sick and tired of disaster and the fools that bring disaster on us."

In the West the Union was winning the war under a general who did not suffer fools gladly: Ulysses S. Grant. Striking through Tennessee toward the Deep South, he handed the North its first strategic success in July 1863: control of the Mississippi River.

That July also brought the Union good news from the East. Lee's invasion of Pennsylvania was stopped short at Gettysburg—and this time his army had been the one forced to limp back across the Potomac River. Confederate Col. Josiah Gorgas had little doubt about what the stunning reverses portended for the rebellion: "The Confederacy totters to its destruction."

"A HOUSE DIVIDED"

We are now far into the fifth year, since a policy was initiated, with the avowed object, and confident promise, of putting an end to slavery agitation. Under the operation of that policy, that agitation has not only not ceased, but has constantly augmented. In my opinion, it will not cease, until a crisis shall have been reached, and passed. A house divided against itself cannot stand. I believe this government cannot endure permanently half slave and half free. I do not expect the Union to be dissolved—I do not expect the house to fall—but I do expect it will cease to be divided. It will become all one thing, or all the other.

–Abraham Lincoln, 1858

Ulysses Simpson Grant, into whose initials admiring Northerners read the words "United States" and "unconditional surrender," arrived in Washington, D.C., in March 1864. The victor of Fort Donelson, Vicksburg, and Chattanooga had come east to assume command of all Union armies in the field and to implement a strategy of total war against the South.

Grant would personally direct operations against Lee's army while Sherman's forces fought and burned their way through Georgia and the Carolinas. "We are not only fighting hostile armies, but a hostile people," wrote Sherman, "and must make old and young, rich and poor, feel the hard hand of war."

Audacious on the attack, superb in defense, General Lee had driven four Union generals from his native state—and from their commands—while leading the Army of Northern Virginia. His men held devout, soft-spoken Lee in awe, even in defeat. "We who live shall never see his like again," a soldier wrote.

If Lee embodied Virginia, his Union counterpart represented pragmatic Yankee stock. Ulysses S. Grant, wrote an officer, "wears an expression as if he had determined to drive his head through a brick wall." Grant's strategy: "Find out where your enemy is, get at him as soon as you can and strike him as hard as you can, and keep moving on."

An enormous Yankee war engine—built by factories and fueled by deficit spending and the labor of immigrants and freed blacks—was arrayed against the South. Railroads shuttled goods and troops through strategic junctions such as Harpers Ferry, West Virginia. Despite its agrarian roots, the Confederacy erected foundries, powder mills, and machine shops, primarily in the Deep South. Confederate armies ran short of butter before guns.

Grant drove hard into Virginia, giving furious battle to Lee in the Wilderness, at Spotsylvania Court House, Cold Harbor, and Petersburg. Lee's army was killing two for every man it lost—but was running out of soldiers. Grant knew the numbers and sensed victory. "I purpose to fight it out on this line if it takes all summer," he wired Lincoln in mid-campaign.

Northern voters reacted to the mounting losses. Grant's "butcher bill," Democrats vowed, would be paid by Lincoln—with his presidency. Their nominee for the 1864 election was the dovish George McClellan, ex-commander of the Army of the Potomac. The South took heart. If Lincoln was ousted, all might yet be well. Confederate raids further sapped Union morale.

Total war claimed its first victim—Meridian, Mississippi—on February 14, 1864. Conquering General Sherman wrote, "Meridian, with its depots, store-houses, arsenals, hospitals, offices, hotels and cantonments no longer exists."

Then electrifying news fatal to McClellan's presidential hopes was telegraphed across the nation: Atlanta had fallen. All but unopposed, Sherman's legions seared a passage to the sea, reaching Savannah shortly before Christmas. "The simple fact that a man's home has been invaded," wrote Sherman, "makes a soldier in Lee's or Johnston's army very, very anxious to get home to look after his family and property." Thousands of Lee's men did just that, as news of Sherman's "hard war" filled desperate letters from home.

The Confederacy was finished, but the war raged on. New seeds of southern bitterness were sown with every farm razed by Sherman, seeds of northern vindictiveness with every boy killed at Petersburg. Reelected, Abraham Lincoln hoped to leave the war's grim harvest unreaped. "With malice toward none; with charity for all," he urged in his Second Inaugural Address, "let us strive on to finish the work we are in; to bind up the nation's wounds." His dream of reuniting the country tragically proved to be unfulfilled. As Lincoln and his wife watched a play at Ford's Theater in Washington, D.C., John Wilkes Booth, a self-described southern patriot, fatally shot him on April 14, 1865.

Lincoln's successor, President Andrew Johnson, a Tennessee Democrat who backed Lincoln's Reconstruction policy, could not win the support of Congress. "Dead men cannot raise themselves," raged Pennsylvania's Thaddeus Stevens. "Dead states cannot restore their existence 'as it was.'" The war had killed 623,000 men. Radical Republicans wanted to punish the South, and Andrew Johnson would be powerless to stop them.

INAUGURAL ADDRESS
FEBRUARY 22, 1862

It is with mingled feelings of humility and pride that I appear to take, in the presence of the people and before high Heaven, the oath prescribed as a qualification for the exalted station to which the unanimous voice of the people has called me . . . The first year in our history has been the most eventful in the annals of this continent. A new government has been established, and its machinery put in operation over an area exceeding seven hundred thousand square miles. The great principles upon which we have been willing to hazard everything that is dear to man have made conquests for us which could never have been achieved by the sword. Our Confederacy has grown from six to thirteen States. . . . Our people have rallied with unexampled unanimity to the support of the great principles of constitutional government, with firm resolve to perpetuate by arms the right which they could not peacefully secure. A million of men, it is estimated, are now standing in hostile array, and waging war along a frontier of thousands of miles...although the contest is not ended, and the tide for the moment is against us, the final result in our favor is not doubtful. . . . With humble gratitude and adoration, acknowledging the Providence which has so visibly protected the Confederacy during its brief but eventful career, to thee, O God, I trustingly commit myself, and prayerfully invoke thy blessing on my country and its cause.

—Jefferson Davis

EMANCIPATION PROCLAMATION

The Beginnings of Freedom for All

"Thenceforward, and forever free." So said President Abraham Lincoln's Emancipation Proclamation on January 1, 1863. The proclamation referred only to slaves in the rebellious states over which Lincoln had no control, so the edict had little actual force. It did however, convert the Civil War into a crusade against slavery, thus making European intervention impossible. It also allowed the Union to recruit black soldiers, nearly 180,000 of whom enlisted during the war.

Before the war, abolitionists worked to end slavery through revealing the demeaning circumstances of the institution. Antislavery meetings, tracts, door-to-door calls, and mailing campaigns made their case through descriptions of life under slavery. The American Anti-Slavery Society alone distributed more than a million pieces of literature in 1835. In 1839 Theodore Dwight Weld, his wife, Angelina, and her sister Sarah Grimké published *American Slavery As It Is*, which drew heavily on eyewitness accounts. Escaped slaves testified at lectures. "I appear . . . this evening as a thief and a robber," Frederick Douglass told an 1842 audience. "I stole this head, these limbs, this body from my master, and ran off with them." The renowned antislavery orator and editor of the *North Star* demanded "emancipation for our enslaved brethren" and the vote for "nominally free" blacks.

In the 1850s, Sojourner Truth fought to end slavery through her speeches. She was born sometime around 1797 in Ulster County, New York, and given the name Isabella Van Wagener. She answered what she felt to be a religious call to "travel up and down the land," so she took the name Sojourner Truth. She became a fervid abolitionist, a powerful preacher, and a strong proponent of the women's rights movement. She sang, debated, and preached wherever she could, at churches, on street corners, at revival meetings.

Moral weapons, however, were blunted by economics and politics. Accounting for three-quarters of the U.S. export trade in 1850, cotton meant wealth—and slavery. The risk of provoking southern secession daunted many politicians. Black leaders despaired of attaining justice in the U.S.; some even countenanced the once heretical idea of emigration to Africa. In the 1850s Martin Delany, an abolitionist editor, declared, "I must admit, that I have no hopes of this country—no confidence in the American people."

Abolitionists tried an old—and ultimately successful—strategy in 1848, after the war with Mexico. They fought to bar the expansion of slavery into the new acquired territories. Pro-slavery forces fought this policy, and the debate would rage through the 1850s. Through involvement in the Free Soil Party and, later the Republican Party, combined with the growing northern feelings against slavery, abolitionists helped provoke the crisis they thought necessary to end slavery.

Although the Emancipation Proclamation did not technically free all the slaves held in the United States, it did mark a turning point in Lincoln's attitude toward the institution. Full rights to citizenship would be granted to all by the 13th, 14th, and 15th Amendments, which were passed after the war's end.

OPPOSITE: *"I Sell the Shadow to Support the Substance," reads a carte-de-visite of Sojourner Truth. The American evangelist and reformer sold the souvenir cards at lectures.*

I Sell the Shadow to Support the Substance.

SOJOURNER TRUTH.

RECONSTRUCTION

Repairing the Union

The defeat of the Confederacy brought suffering as well as freedom to the South's former slaves. During the war, many had followed Union troops, camping in makeshift shacks, often sick and starving. Others looked for family members lost in the confusion of war.

But the fate of the eleven former states remained uncertain. How could they be brought back into the Union? For residents of these states, answers were difficult to find. "We are scattered—stunned—the remnant of heart left alive within us, filled with brotherly hate. We sit and wait until the drunken tailor who rules . . . issues a proclamation and defines our anomalous position," Mary Boykin Chesnut of South Carolina wrote of Lincoln's successor, President Andrew Johnson. Civil War was over, civil strife was not.

Yet Johnson was the white South's best ally. He led a minority coalition to seek a lenient peace that accorded dignity to the South. His opponents, Radical Republicans led by Thaddeus Stevens and Charles Sumner, did not trust white Southerners and northern Democrats to grant blacks equality. As proof they cited race riots in Memphis and New Orleans and newly enacted repressive "black codes."

In the battle of Reconstruction, Johnson called three Radical Republicans "traitors." Even

the President's supporters were appalled by such abrasive behavior. A Republican Congress passed the Civil Rights Act and other laws over his veto. In 1868 the House impeached him; Johnson was spared removal by one vote in the Senate.

Ulysses S. Grant, winner of the presidential election of 1868, had far less success as a politician than as a general. His administration proved inept in dealing with economic turmoil and ineffective in coping with a united white front in the South.

Congress grew stronger, and the Radical Republicans who dominated it succeeded in passing legislation that divided the remaining ten Southern states (Tennessee had been readmitted in 1866) into military districts controlled by the U.S. Army. A state could only be readmitted by accepting the 14th and 15th Amendments, passed to guarantee the rights of ex-slaves. Arkansas, North Carolina, Alabama, Florida, Louisiana, and South Carolina rejoined in 1868. Last were Virginia, Mississippi, Texas, and Georgia in 1870.

A NEW BEGINNING

After the Civil War's end, three amendments to the Constituion ended slavery, defined U.S. citizenship, and ensured the rights of all people.

Amendment XIII, Section I. Neither slavery nor involuntary servitude, except as a punishment for crime whereof the party shall have been duly convicted, shall exist within the United States, or any place subject to their jurisdiction.

Amendment XIV, Section I. All persons born or naturalized in the United States . . . are citizens of the United States and of the state wherein they reside. No state shall make or enforce any law which shall abridge the privileges or immunities of citizens of the United States; nor shall any state deprive any person of life, liberty, or property, without due process of law; nor deny to any person within its jurisdiction the equal protection of the laws.

Amendment XV, Section I. The right of citizens of the United States to vote shall not be denied or abridged by the United States or by any state on account of race, color, or previous condition of servitude. ■

After the war, three groups came to power in the Southern state governments: One consisted of northerners who had moved south, some to help rebuild the region, some to make their own fortunes. Many carried suitcases made of carpet material—so were called "carpetbaggers." Also in power were southerners who had opposed secession, called "scalawags," and newly enfranchised blacks. Most former Confederates opposed them.

Standing between freed blacks and southern whites were agents of the Bureau of Refugees, Freedmen, and Abandoned Lands, who worked to ease the transition from slavery to freedom. Though it made gains in labor relations and education for blacks, the bureau was plagued by lack of staff and by insufficient funds, and in many states it was actively opposed by the Ku Klux Klan. Founded in early 1866 in Pulaski, Tennessee, by six former Confederate soldiers, the Klan killed black political leaders and burned Freedmen's Bureau schoolhouses. The bureau was dismantled by Congress in 1872, having fallen short of most of its major objectives.

The 1876 presidential election was the final blow to Reconstruction. Republican Rutherford B. Hayes lost the popular vote to Samuel J. Tilden but won an electoral college victory by promising to remove troops from the South. Occupation of the South represented a compromise within the factious Republican Party. The intent was to coerce state governments into recognizing black political equality and accepting the 14th Amendment—the central requirement for readmission to the Union. When the last federal troops left in 1877, with them went realistic hopes for racial equality.

As a policy of enforcing equal rights in the South, Reconstruction was dead. The 13th, 14th, and 15th Amendments to the Constitution and the Civil Rights Acts of 1866 and 1875 were alive, but only on paper.

OPPOSITE: *The old South—and the new: In Georgia in the 1860s, Spanish moss dangles above two African American women, newly freed.*

The RAILROADS

Webs of Transportation

In 1826, Baltimore's merchants, bankers, and lawyers met to discuss a new technology that seemed to promise economic prosperity for their city: the railroad. They founded the Baltimore and Ohio Railroad Company, the first U.S. steam-operated railway to carry freight and passengers.

Railroads had been developed in Europe. But imported English locomotives could not pull heavy loads, and light-gauge tracks buckled under their weight. Underpowered and overweight locomotives might suffice in Britain, perhaps, which could afford to build expensive roadbeds for them. But American railroad companies had enormous distances to span and little money to spend. By the mid-1830s locomotives made by American master mechanics were at work on the B & O and scores of other railroads. Strong and lightweight, able to run on inexpensive track, they established America's reputation as a world leader in locomotive engineering.

In 1830 South Carolina pioneered steam passenger rail service in the U.S. and three years later completed a 135-mile railroad, then the world's longest. Connection with the Georgia Railroad transformed Terminus—renamed Atlanta in 1847—into the South's premier rail hub.

By 1852 the B & O and three other northern railroads extended beyond the Appalachians. There they bought the disjointed system of midwestern railroads already in place and began building. The B & O pioneered connections to St. Louis and Cincinnati, the Pennsylvania Railroad to Dayton and Indianapolis. The richest prize, Chicago, first was connected to the East in February 1852. Grange railroads fanned out from hub cities to bring crops to market. In the South, railroads made Richmond, Atlanta, Memphis, and Chattanooga entrepôts for tobacco and cotton—and objects of Union attack during the Civil War.

By 1860, 30,500 miles of railroad track had been laid—almost as much as the rest of the world combined. Two-thirds of it was in the North. While many railroads ran east and west, only three linked the North to the South in 1860. Eleven railroads met in Chicago, already the nation's rail hub. In 1862 Abraham Lincoln, anxious to cement California in the Union, signed into existence the Union Pacific Railroad and ordered it to link with the Central Pacific between Omaha and Sacramento.

The Union Pacific brought in more than 10,000 men. Most were Irish immigrants, some of them Civil War veterans. In California the Central Pacific recruited more than 10,000 Chinese immigrants to build its part of the line. Some had come to California because of the discovery of gold in 1848, but many had come to find jobs, planning to return home with the wages earned. Armed with picks, shovels, and sledgehammers, the railroad workers cleared and leveled land for the track.

On May 10, 1869, two locomotives stood nose to nose on tracks stretching to opposite horizons, "half a world behind each back," as a San Francisco editor put it. Bandmaster Capt. Charles Currier's description ended on a sober note: "Thus is the greatest undertaking of the 19th century accomplished. All honors to the resolute men who have 'put it through.'"

By 1883 four railroads crossed the West, making tracks for Dakota wheat fields, Rocky Mountain mining towns, California farmland, and Washington state timber; hauling out raw resources; and hauling in money, settlers, and goods.

Railroading's golden age was under way. Pullman cars crossed the Great Plains, passengers leaning from windows to gaze at herds of buffalo.

May 2. Sunday.—Scott today went forward and gave his name to the church with half a dozen of his cronies. I think the step tends to hedge him round with good influences. He needs them as little as anybody of his age; but all boys need such restraining and pure influence.

It may be truly said that for twenty-five years, at least, railroad workingmen have had too little, and railroad capitalists and managers, those who have controlled and manipulated railroads, have had too much of their earnings—or too much of the money made out of them. The public has been neglected; its rights and interests disregarded. Not men enough employed—not paid enough—etc., etc.

The railroads should be under a wise, watchful, and powerful supervision by the Government. No violence, no lawlessness, destructive of life and property, should be allowed. It should be suppressed instantly and with a strong hand. A bucket of water at the beginning will put out a fire which if neglected will burn up the city. There is no sense, there is no humanity in hesitation of [or] temporizing.

–Rutherford B. Hayes, 1886
19th President of the United States
(1871–1881)

Trains like the Empire State Express set standards of opulence and thrilled the public with full-throttle runs at record speeds.

Trains ran on time. Americans could literally set their watches by them—first by choice, then by law. It is thanks to the railroad schedules that eastern, central, mountain, and Pacific timezones came into existence. A Canadian railway engineer devised a plan for standard time, adopted by the U.S. and 26 other nations in 1884. Terminals like New York's Grand Central were monuments to efficiency. "Through this new gateway . . . ," the New York Times stated in 1913, "the entire population of the United States could pass in a single year without crowding and without confusion."

ABOVE: *Photographed sometime between 1865 and 1869, workers stand by stacked timbers along the tracks on the Central Pacific Railroad.*

NEXT: *A crew on the Northern Pacific Railroad takes a break somewhere in the American West. Crews could be diverse, with Irish, Chinese, and Mexicans working alongside one another. In carefully choreographed moves, they pounded ties and plates into position. Then 12 men hoisted heavy, 30-foot-long rails into place. Spike drivers hit each spike three times—there were ten spikes to a rail—and America crept westward.*

AMERICAN WEST

Life on the Frontier

Cattle crossed the Appalachians with settlers in the late 1700s. Cattle herding as a large-scale operation began early among British colonists on the Eastern Seaboard, particularly in South Carolina, and moved west over major migration routes. Anglo-style open-range techniques in the East, including branding and dog herding, blended with the Hispanic roping and riding styles of Louisiana and eastern Texas to produce a new ranching system that spread through the Great Plains. As early as the 1840s hundreds of thousands of longhorns grazed in Texas. At first the lanky cattle were valued only for hides, tallow, hooves, and horns.

During the Civil War, Chicago stockyards provisioned the Union Army. After the war's end, these stockyards were taken over for commercial purposes. Demand rose in the East for meat, and it became profitable for Texans to drive herds north on such trails as the Chisholm to stops along the Kansas Pacific Railroad. From there they were transshipped to markets.

During the 1870s and 1880s Texas cattlemen sent millions of head north on long drives to grasslands or railheads. It is from these cattledrives that the cowboy was born. Ranch hands rode the range for months at a time— from April "till the wagon made tracks through four-inch Christmas snow," according to one wife. At the end of the trail, cattle crowded the stockyards of East St. Louis, Omaha, Abilene, Kansas City, and Chicago.

Every bit of a cowboy's equipment reflected active life under the open skies. His small, tough,

sure-footed horse, a descendant of Spanish stock, could carry him 30 to 40 miles a day. His wide-brimmed hat protected him from the sun—and doubled as a pillow or water bucket. His bandanna, worn as a mask, kept him from choking when riding dusty trails. Heavy leather chaps protected his legs in brushy country; gloves and cuffs helped prevent rope burn when working with his lasso. His vest provided handy pockets; a slicker, carried behind his saddle, kept him dry in the rain—and was useful at night as a ground cloth. High-heeled boots held the stirrups. His gun could be used as a signal or a defense against rattlesnakes and rustlers.

Between the 1860s and 1890s, as more ranchers, farmers, and sheepherders moved west, contests for rights to grazing lands from the Texas Panhandle to the Dakotas turned bitter. Cattlemen seized both public and Indian lands and wrote their own laws. Associations of stockmen briefly became unauthorized governments in the territories. Cattle companies strung barbed-wire fences around millions of acres of grazing land and shut out small farmers and ranchers from watercourses. In 1883 a Galveston newspaper reported that 20 miles of barbed-wire fence on the property of the Hickey Pasture Company had been cut to bits, presumably by neighbors who refused to be denied a handy water supply. The first commercially successful barbed wire—there were eventually hundreds of types—was introduced in 1874 by an Illinois farmer and inventor, Joseph F. Glidden. His most notable design, the Winner, had double-twist barbs on two strands of wire.

The fencing cost $100 to $200 a mile but paid for itself; ranchers needed fewer hands to care for cattle, and stock was kept from straying. As much as any six-shooter, barbed wire inflamed western conflicts. For more than a decade, fence wars flared. "Range hogs" and cattle barons hired gunmen to protect their fences, while unlikely alliances of rangers, farmers, and cattle drivers armed with wire cutters fought for open access to the land well into the 1890s.

Farmers and ranchers were willing to buy unwatered land, then enclose it and drill wells as deep as 800 feet. Well water pumped by windmills into reservoirs allowed ranchers to safeguard against drought and to spread herds (which stuck close to water) over a much wider range.

During this unsettled time, the West was a violent place. Sometimes it was hard to tell the good from the bad, as they often had more in common than not—men with high spirits and low morals. When they disagreed or had a score to settle, it was easy to reach for a gun. Law and order lagged behind the westward advance of civilization, and the frontier was the home of itinerant cowboys, prospectors, railroad men, fugitives, and con artists.

Most fearsome of the western gunfighters were the men who rode in gangs—like the James brothers, Jesse and Frank. They robbed banks,

FROM *THE VIRGINIAN*

It was now the Virginian's turn to bet, or leave the game, and he did not speak at once. Therefore Trampas spoke. "Your bet, you son-of-a- —."

The Virginian's pistol came out, and his hand lay on the table, holding it unaimed. And with a voice as gentle as ever, the voice that sounded almost like a caress, but drawling a very little more than usual . . . he issued his orders to the man Trampas: "When you call me that, SMILE." And he looked at Trampas across the table. Yes, the voice was gentle. But in my ears it seemed as if somewhere the bell of death was ringing; and silence, like a stroke, fell on the large room . . . Then, with equal suddenness and ease, the room came out of its strangeness. Voices and cards, the click of chips, the puff of tobacco, glasses lifted to drink: This level of smooth relaxation hinted no more plainly of what lay beneath than does the surface tell the depth of the sea. For Trampas had made his choice. And that choice was not to "draw his steel."

—Owen Wister

OPPOSITE: *Frederic Remington created this romantic image of the West ca 1904. Breaking horses was part of a cowboy's job, as the horse played a vital role in transporting herds of cattle to market.*

trains, and stagecoaches. They had learned about hit-and-run raids during their years in Confederate guerrilla bands during the Civil War, when they preyed upon Union troops along the Kansas–Missouri border. With peace, the James brothers organized a band that numbered as many as a dozen men. They planned their assaults carefully and struck swiftly, then vanished. The James gang flourished for 15 years, from 1866 to 1881, executing 26 raids in and around Missouri. They stole an estimated half a million dollars.

The James Gang's adventures ended in Northfield, Minnesota, when a bungled 1876 bank robbery roused the town's citizens into fighting back and destroying the gang. Jesse and Frank, however, escaped to the Dakota Territory.

A LETTER FROM BILLY THE KID

I wrote You a little note the day before yesterday but have received no answer. I Expect you have forgotten what you promised me, this Month two Years ago, but I have not, and I think You had ought to have come and seen me as I requested you to. I have done everything that I promised you I would, and You have done nothing You promised me.

I think that when You think The matter over, You will come down and See me, and I can then Explain Everything to you.

Judge Leonard, Passed through here on his way East, and promised to come and See me on his way back, but he did not fulfil his Promise. It looks to me like I am getting left in the Cold. I am not treated right by [Marshall] Sherman, he lets Every Stranger that comes to See me through Curiosity in to see me, but will not let a Single one of my friends in, not Even an Attorney.

I guess they mean to Send me up without giving me any Show but they will have a nice time doing it. I am not intirely without friends.

I shall expect to see you some time today.
Patiently waiting
I am Very truly Yours, Respt.
W. H. Bonney
　　—Sent to New Mexico Governor Lew Wallace, from the Santa Fe Jail, March 4, 1881

Charged with keeping order in frontier towns were lawmen variously known as town marshal, county sheriff, state or territorial ranger, or federal marshal. Sheriff Bat Masterson called them "just plain ordinary men who could shoot straight and had the most utter courage and perfect nerve—and, for the most part, a keen sense of right and wrong." Arrests were not always as colorful as portrayed in Westerns. In a typical month in Tombstone, Arizona, Virgil Earp and his deputies made 48 arrests, of which only eight involved violence. Of these, 18 were drunk-and-disorderly charges, and 14 were for disturbing the peace.

There were also those officers who maintained second careers as practicing outlaws. The citizens of Laramie, Wyoming, hanged their head lawman when they discovered that in his capacity as saloonkeeper he was drugging and robbing his patrons. Similarly, vigilantes hanged the sheriff of Ada County, Idaho, when he was found to be a horse thief.

For a while, justice in the courtrooms was as hit-or-miss as in the jails and on the streets. Many early judges lacked a formal legal education and were often tradesmen on the side. Without courthouses and courtrooms, they dispensed justice in stores or saloons. An especially colorful figure was Judge Phantly "Roy" Bean, who was born in Mason County, Kentucky, sometime around 1825. While still a teenager he and his brother hitched onto a wagon train to New Mexico, then spent several years wandering from town to town.

By 1882 he was west of the Pecos River running a bar, the Jersey Lilly. He lacked a real education but persuaded the Texas Rangers to set him up as a Justice of the Peace. He began administering his form of eccentric justice with just one lawbook, *The Revised Statutes of Texas*, in 1879. His rulings, it was said, were "characterized by greed, prejudice, a little common sense and lots of colorful language." Judge Bean died in 1903.

RIGHT: *Founder of the popular Wild West Show, William Frederick "Buffalo Bill" Cody kneels on the right, wearing a buckskin outfit and carrying a rifle.*

FORGING *the* FURURE

Steel and Steelmen

In the early 1850s, William Kelly developed a process to make soft, malleable steel without consuming volumes of charcoal. He failed to patent his work, so an Englishman, Henry Bessemer, gained fame and the British and U.S. patents for his own version of the process. Alexander Holley ushered in modern American steelmaking in 1865, designing the nation's first

Bessemer plant at Troy, New York. In 1890 the U.S. passed Great Britain as top steel producer.

Fiery 15-minute blasts of Bessemer converters signaled the end of iron's 3,000-year reign and the emergence of steel, whose output was to be in thousands of tons. The open-hearth furnace, developed in Europe and refined in the U.S. during the 1880s, boosted yearly output to millions of tons. It also removed phosphorus better than the Bessemer process, enabling greater use of the phosphorus-rich ore of the massive Great Lakes ranges and creating a stronger grade of steel.

When anthracite coal began replacing charcoal as fuel in the 1830s, iron makers left rural iron plantations to locate furnaces near coal deposits. Cheaper transportation and demand for raw materials brought the mining of bituminous coal and led to larger, integrated manufacturing units. The eventual result was an industrial complex of mines, ships, railroads, and steel plants. "Hell with the lid taken off," wrote a visitor to Pittsburgh in 1868.

Commanding three rivers and surrounded by coal, Pittsburgh became the early center of iron and steel manufacturing. By 1904, 34 separate iron-and-steel plants lined Pittsburgh's rivers. U.S. Steel owned two-thirds of both the plants'

capacity, wielding such power that it established a pricing system—Pittsburgh Plus—that dominated the entire industry until 1948. Working in a steel mill was dangerous. During the 12-hour turns at the open hearth, scrap metal might jam and 20-ton ladles spatter molten bullets.

The industry grew in a helter-skelter fashion, and eventually some 800 plants fed America's appetite for steel. Andrew Carnegie's was by far the largest but, at age 65, Carnegie wanted a new life of philanthropy and ease. The stage was set for the creation of the country's first billion-dollar corporation: U.S. Steel.

Famed banker J. P. Morgan brokered the deal, on January 6, 1901, in his library at 219 Madison Avenue in New York City. Present were a representative of Carnegie; the controller of American Steel and Wire; and Morgan's partner, Robert Bacon. They consolidated those 800 steel plants into a single company that would mine iron ore at one end and spew out all the finished steel the country could need at the other.

The creation of U.S. Steel was the climax of the most massive and rapid burst of industrial concentration the world had ever seen. Between 1879 and 1897 there had been only 12 U.S. "combinations" with a total capitalization of one billion dollars. A "combination" was the process whereby great interstate corporations, or "trusts," and later holding companies, were created and centrally administered by directors answerable only to the loose laws of a local entity, such as a small state. Their creation led to the enforcement, by Theodore Roosevelt, the "trust buster," of the Sherman Anti-Trust Act of 1890. Other industrialists, like John

MAP Showing THE PROPERTIES OF The UNITED STATES STEEL CORPORATION.

PUBLISHED BY WHITE & KEMBLE, 41 EXCHANGE PLACE, NEW YORK

ANDREW CARNEGIE

As a 13-year-old Scottish immigrant, Andrew Carnegie worked in a textile factory for $1.20 a week, but by 1901, when he sold his steel mill for $480 million, he was the wealthiest man in the world. He founded the J. Edgar Thomson Steel Works near Pittsburgh, which eventually evolved into the Carnegie Steel Company. He built the first steel plants in the U.S. to use the new Bessemer system; detailed cost- and production-accounting procedures enabled the company to achieve great efficiencies. In the 1890s his mills introduced the basic open-hearth furnace into American steelmaking. By 1889 the Carnegie Steel Company dominated the American steel industry. But Carnegie believed that a "man who dies rich dies disgraced," so after 1900 he devoted his life to giving away his fortune. All told, his trusts have given away some $350 million, both in Britain and the U.S. His money founded 281 public libraries all over America, among other charities. ■

D. Rockefeller, John Jacob Astor, and Cornelius Vanderbilt, all came to be known by the pejorative nickname "robber barons" for their abilities to gain enormous wealth and power.

Morgan's consolidation of U.S. Steel marked another new trend in American business: The robber barons were turning over their massive businesses to bankers and stock promoters. These financial professionals, like Morgan, knew nothing of the individual industries they were controlling. They knew Business.

OPPOSITE: *With the White House in the palm of his hand, John D. Rockefeller controls both Washington and the oil market, according to an early cartoon. In the distance, government buildings appear as a part of his company, Standard Oil.*

ABOVE: *U.S. Steel used color coding in a 1903 map to distinguish its rail and steamship lines, iron ranges, coal and gas fields, smelters, and other properties.*

ORGANIZING *the* WORKERS

Labor and Unionization

The 1876 Centennial Exposition in Philadelphia celebrated everything American, except her workers. Few visitors who marveled at the Corliss steam engine noticed its lone operator. But William Dean Howells did. He observed: "Now and then he lays down his [news]paper and clambers up one of the stairways . . . and touches some irritated spot on the giant's body with a drop of oil." The exposition proclaimed the future, a vision that did not admit the army of carpenters, pickax men, and masons who had transformed its 284 acres in less than two years.

Railroad workers were less easily forgotten. Stunned the following summer by a 10 percent pay cut, their third since a depression hit in 1873, workers on the Baltimore and Ohio line went on strike. Soon other lines struck, as did sympathetic factory workers and miners. Ordered to guard property, West Virginia militiamen refused to fire on the strikers and were replaced by federal troops. Rioting spread to Pittsburgh and Chicago. By the end of July rail yards across the country lay smoldering, and more than a hundred people lay dead.

The rail strike was broken, but the sympathy strikes signaled a growing cohesiveness among industrial workers. Work stoppages generally followed business cycles, increasing during periods of prosperity and diminishing when business activity declined and jobs disappeared. Samuel Gompers in 1881 began uniting craft unions and fighting for immediate economic goals. By 1900 his American Federation of Labor (AFL) spoke for most of the labor movement.

Confronting giant corporations and trusts—in sugar, steel, tobacco, and oil—workers in the 1880s increased efforts to organize nationally. Employers fought these "muscle trusts" with injunctions, lockouts, blacklists, and armed guards. From 1865 to 1881 labor had staged fewer than 500 strikes to press its demands. Between 1881 and 1894 there were 14,900 strikes, involving four million workers.

The International Ladies' Garment Workers' Union was founded in 1900; they had already won concessions by 1912. A three-month strike that began in 1909 gained a 52-hour workweek and wage increases. Women often worked up to 14 hours a day in tenement lofts or in the city's thousands of "home factories." Shunned by some unions, women were actively recruited by others, including the well-known Terence Powderly's Knights of Labor, which had chartered 192 women's assemblies by 1886.

Black workers had far less success than women did in gaining acceptance into labor unions. Some unions had racial restrictions; others offered only segregated affiliation. Employers undermined organized labor in the early 1900s by recruiting southern blacks to come to northern cities as strikebreakers. A. Philip Randolph gained new respect for blacks among unionists by organizing the Brotherhood of Sleeping Car Porters and winning national attention in 1928 with a threatened strike. Gradually responding to the Congress of Industrial Organization's (CIO's) aggressive recruiting, blacks began joining unions in substantial numbers in the 1930s.

Mass-production workers went largely unrepresented until John L. Lewis broke away in 1938 and organized entire industries under the CIO. Yet the organization of labor had to fight business opposition every step of the way.

Rising affluence and legislation protecting the rights of workers gradually changed the battlefront from picket lines to bargaining tables. Fringe benefits such as medical care and tuition credits became part of complex agreements.

THE AMERICAN RED CROSS

"If Heaven ever sent out a holy angel, she must be one," wrote a surgeon of Clara Barton. She first gained fame for nursing the wounded on battlefields, then expanded to offer relief to the civilian victims of warfare.

Fittingly, she was a Christmas baby, born on Christmas Day in 1821 in Oxford, Massachusetts. By 15 she was a teacher. She first found a way to be of assistance during the Civil War, when she helped track and recover soldiers' lost baggage. After the first Battle of Bull Run she rounded up medicines and supplies for the wounded and even persuaded authorities to let her pass through the lines to search for missing soldiers, to pass out supplies, to succor the wounded. She had found her calling and carried on with relief work throughout the war.

She was vacationing in Europe when the Franco-German War broke out, and she again sprang into action organizing relief work for victims. In Europe she worked with the International Red Cross and, when she returned home, urged the U.S. to sign the Geneva Conventions. She founded the American Red Cross in 1881 and served as its president until 1904.

When soldiers in Cuba fighting the Spanish American war needed her, she was there, at age 77. But she grew more controlling as she aged, jealous of interference, authoritarian, and reluctant to cede any power. Still, her accomplishments survive, and she was often called the "angel of the battlefield." She died in Glen Echo, Maryland, on April 12, 1912. ∎

OPPOSITE: *Signs of protest, in several languages, appear at the picket line of a garment workers' union strike in New York City around 1912. Shorter hours and higher pay were often the chief goals of early unions.*

NATIONAL PARKS

Protecting Wild America

Artist George Catlin, on a trip to the Dakotas in 1832, worried about the impact of America's westward expansion on Indian tribes, wildlife, and wilderness. They might be preserved, he thought, "by some great protecting policy of government . . . in a magnificent park . . . A nation's park, containing man and beast, in all the wild and freshness of their nature's beauty!"

His vision was partly realized in 1864 when Congress donated Yosemite Valley to California

as a state park. The Park embraces a spectacular tract of mountain-and-valley scenery in the Sierra Nevadas, with waterfalls, meadows, and forests, including groves of giant sequoias.

The move to preserve the wild lands continued when Jim Bridger invited a credulous colleague to "come with me to the Yellowstone next summer, and I'll show you peetrified trees a-growing, with peetrified birds on 'em a-singing peetrified songs." Bridger also had serious tales for more serious ears, and he undertook three expeditions, in 1869, 1870, and 1871, to separate Yellowstone fact from fiction.

Even a mountain man's embellishments could scarcely top what they found: explosive geysers, mud volcanoes, scalding springs—one of the densest regions of thermal activity in the world. In 1872 Congress officially recognized the uniqueness of the area, passing "An Act to set apart a certain Tract of Land lying near the Headwaters of the Yellowstone River as a public Park." This Wyoming tract would be not only the nation's first national park but also the world's.

Fittingly, the first national memorial honored Ulysses S. Grant, who had signed the act establishing the first national park, Yellowstone, on March 1, 1872. Some 90,000 people donated more than $600,000 toward construction of the memorial, and in 1897 it was completed. Grant's Tomb, where both he and his wife, Julia Dent Grant, lie, was dedicated on April 27, 1897, and is still managed by the National Park Service.

The same year that Congress created the General Grant Memorial, it also established Sequoia National Park in California. But as there was not yet a National Park Service to administer parks, cavalry troops protected the big trees, and each year a company cantered out from San Francisco's Presidio to police the park.

JOHN MUIR

Nature is a good mother," he wrote, "and sees well to the clothing of her many bairns—birds with imbricated feathers, beetles with shining jackets, and bears with shaggy furs. In the south, where the sun warms like a fire, they are allowed to go thinly clad; in the north-land she takes care to clothe warmly."

He was born in Scotland but became one of America's most eloquent spokesmen for her wild treasures and lands. He emigrated from Scotland with his family to a farm near Portage, Wisconsin, in 1849, studied at the University of Wisconsin, and worked on mechanical inventions. But in 1867 an accident nearly cost him an eye, and he abandoned his career to thereafter devote himself to nature. He walked to the Gulf of Mexico and wrote a book about it: A Thousand-Mile Walk to the Gulf. In 1868 he went to Yosemite Valley in California and from there traveled into Nevada, Utah, Oregon, Washington, and Alaska, studying glaciers and forests.

By 1876 he was urging the federal government to adopt a forest conservation policy, and, given impetus by two eloquent magazine articles in June and August 1897, he swung public and congressional opinion in favor of national forest reserves.

In 1908 the federal government established the Muir Woods National Monument in Marin County, California. Muir died in Los Angeles on Christmas Eve, 1914. ∎

After the establishment of Yellowstone National Park in 1872, conservation milestones began to occur regularly. That same year saw the first observance in Nebraska of Tree-Planting Day on April 10, which soon became Arbor Day. A year later Franklin B. Hough addressed the annual meeting of the American Association for the Advancement of Science and read his paper, "On the Duty of Governments in the Preservation of Forests." New York in 1885 proclaimed that the state's Adirondack Mountains "shall be kept forever as wild forest lands." In 1889 William Temple Hornaday published a report to the Secretary of the Smithsonian Institution called "The Extermination of the American Bison"; it chronicled their near extinction. Americans began to recognize the importance of the sites and artifacts of the country's Native Americans late in the 19th century; Arizona's Casa Grande Ruin was the first such site to be protected by Congress, in 1889.

President Theodore Roosevelt tripled the nation's forest reserves' size to 150 million acres, although his goal was conservation of resources, not preservation of wilderness.

By 1916 there were 37 national parks and monuments, and responsibility for them was turned over to the Department of the Interior. President Woodrow Wilson signed the act creating the National Park Service on August 25. The act called for those parks and others yet to be named to remain "unimpaired for the enjoyment of future generations."

ABOVE: *President Theodore Roosevelt and conservationist John Muir stand above Yosemite Valley, California, circa 1900. Both fought to protect America's natural landscape and to preserve its wildlands.*
NEXT: *As it works its way through the Grand Canyon National Park, the mighty Colorado River reflects the sky and clouds.*

The TELEGRAPH and TELEPHONE

Lines of Communication

The first transatlantic calls were made by radio in 1927, and a cable was laid in 1956. In 1969 the first earth-to-moon call was placed, and by the 1970s calling the other side of the world via satellite had become routine.

The telephone had its origins in the telegraph, invented by Samuel F. B. Morse, a New York professor. He and his partner, Alfred Vail, transmitted the first message, "What hath God wrought!" on May 24, 1844, and inaugurated a new age. Newspapers quickly

learned to use the new tool to transmit news from anywhere in the country, and in 1848 the Associated Press was formed. By mid-century more than 50 telegraph companies were making the wires hum in the U.S. Several of them joined together in 1856 to form the Western Union Telegraph Company. Its first coast-to-coast line was completed in 1861. The telegraph showed that sounds could travel over wires. Alexander Graham Bell was listening.

Bell exhibited his telephone at the 1876 Centennial Exposition in Philadelphia. Though primitive, it did well enough when Bell recited Hamlet's "To be or not to be" soliloquy into the instrument at one end of the hall with Dom Pedro II, Emperor of Brazil, listening at the other. The monarch exclaimed, "I hear, I hear."

One year after Bell's first phone call, the Bell Telephone Company was established in Boston.

More than 600 subscribers signed up despite early technical problems, including the need for "occasional repetition" to get a message through. Each private line was connected to only two or three other points. That design limitation, however, was soon remedied, and the first central exchange connected 21 subscribers of New Haven, Connecticut, in 1878. Bell resigned from the phone company in 1880 and used his profits to finance other inventions and work with the deaf.

For the user, the telephone's greatest asset was its simplicity. It required no knowledge of codes, no dexterity, only speech. By 1881, 132,692 Bell telephones were in service, and only nine cities with populations over 10,000 were without a telephone exchange. A decade after the telephone was introduced to the world, a Manhattan telephone pole might hold as many as 300 wires, each of which could carry only one call at a time. Growing outrage in New York City over the eyesore of overhead wires led to efforts as early as the 1880s to bury them underground in insulated cables. By then more than 180,000 subscribers were linked by at least as many miles of copper wire.

Doctors, retailers, and other businessmen owned most phones, and monthly service cost more than half of the average worker's income. Rates were high—as much as $150 a year for business phones, $100 for residential. In 1919 a

three-minute coast-to-coast call cost $16.50, more than $100 today.

Independent telephone companies, freed by the 1894 expiration of Bell's original patents, extended service to rural areas. By 1907 the greatest concentration of telephones per person was not in the East but in Iowa, Nebraska, Washington, and California. To gain residential customers, the telephone industry promoted practical uses such as ordering groceries and calling doctors. Only after World War I did the industry fully recognize the profit potential of encouraging people to chat with family and friends.

After 1890 a long-distance network grew steadily from its New England base, pushing west to Chicago by 1893. Expansion was boosted in 1900 with development of the loading coil, which reduced weakening of the long-distance signal. AT&T dominated toll lines, denying independent firms access to them until 1913. Another technological milestone, electronic repeaters to amplify signals, made possible the first transcontinental line, opened between New York and San Francisco in 1915. By 1914 ten million telephones—70 percent of the world's total—were in the U.S.; by 1916 more than 70,000 communities were linked to the network.

OPPOSITE: *Just a few years after Bell's invention, wires needed for his apparatus crosshatch lower Broadway. After 1900, underground routing buried most of them.*
ABOVE: *In 1892, Alexander Graham Bell makes the first telephone call from New York to Chicago.*

1900

THROUGH

1949

A NATION *at* WAR

M ECHANIZED AMERICA THUNDERED INTO the 20th century, inventing, building, and sometimes breaking down. "We guess a trestle will stand forever," a rail passenger told his aghast fellow traveler, Rudyard Kipling, before crossing a flimsy-looking bridge. "And sometimes we guess ourselves into the depot, and sometimes we guess ourselves into Hell." Confidently bridging the oceans with its institutions, the U.S. guessed itself into possessions in the Caribbean and the Pacific. In 1916, President Woodrow Wilson worked to keep the U.S. out of Europe's Great War, worried that the country might grow "divided in camps of hostile opinion, hot against each other."

But the U.S. inevitably became involved, and by World War I's end, the U.S. was half rural, half urban, citifying fast, and a new world power to boot. Trains gave way to cars and planes and construction soared skyward as engineers built with new materials—and new visions. Radio gained listeners all over the world, and in the corner cinema, moving pictures learned to talk.

Women joined men at the polls. Immigrants poured into America from other countries. Some Americans paused to give a helping hand to the exploited and the less fortunate. Labor unions fought for power while industry grew. The good times rolled. But everything came crashing down in the grim 1930s, and it would take another world war to put it all back together again. An apocalyptic new force, created by splitting tiny atoms, illuminated mid-century; it would hover over Americans for their foreseeable future.

On D-Day, June 6, 1944, American soldiers wade toward the beach at Normandy, France.

PIONEERs *of* AVIATION

~

Taking to the Skies

"To fly, to fly—it was the oldest of dreams . . . ," intoned historian David McCullough, host of a television documentary about the Wright Brothers. "And then one day it happened. Early in the new twentieth century at a remote spot on the outer coast of North Carolina, two young unknown Americans, brothers from Dayton, Ohio, succeeded as no human beings ever had. First one, then the other took off and landed in a flying machine—wings, propeller, gasoline engine, all of their own design. It was astounding."

The bachelor brothers lived at home with their preacher father in Dayton, where they ran a shop that built and repaired bicycles. They were unassuming midwestern young men, but, "while self-taught, were exceedingly serious aeronautical engineers—painstaking, resourceful, highly creative, truly brilliant and brave." History gives them credit for accomplishing the world's first powered, sustained, and controlled airplane flight in 1903 and followed that with the first fully practical airplane flight in 1905.

They went about it systematically in their workshop and on the beach at North Carolina, first experimenting with a series of gliders, then solving the problems of lift and control, and finally achieving powered, sustained flight. But others around the world were working on the same problems, and Orville and Wilbur devoted most of the rest of their lives to trying to make money from their invention and protecting their patents from others.

Another aviation pioneer was Charles A. Lindbergh, who made the first nonstop solo flight across the Atlantic Ocean, from New York to Paris, on May 20-21, 1927. He was born in 1902 and grew up largely in Little Falls, Minnesota, and in Washington, D.C., where his father was a U.S. congressman. He purchased a World War I Curtiss Jenny—his first plane—and in 1926 began flying the mail between St. Louis and Chicago. Several wealthy St. Louis businessmen put up the money that made it possible for him to compete for a prize that was being offered—$25,000 to the pilot who made the first successful nonstop flight between New York and Paris. In the simple, boxy monoplane *Spirit of St. Louis* he set off for Europe.

On his way, he wrote, "Now I've burned the last bridge behind me. All through the storm and darkest night, my instincts were anchored to the continent of North America, as though an invisi-

---

ON LEARNING TO FLY AN AIRPLANE

Now, there are two ways of learning how to ride a fractious horse: one is to get on him and learn by actual practice how each motion and trick may be best met; the other is to sit on a fence and watch the beast a while, and then retire to the house and at leisure figure out the best way of overcoming his jumps and kicks. The latter system is the safest; but the former, on the whole, turns out the larger proportion of good riders. It is very much the same in learning to ride a flying machine; if you are looking for perfect safety, you will do well to sit on a fence and watch the birds; but if you really wish to learn, you must mount a machine and become acquainted with its tricks by actual trial.

–Wilbur Wright

ble cord still tied me to its coasts. In an emergency—if the ice-filled clouds had merged, if oil pressure had begun to drop, if a cylinder had started missing—I should have turned back toward America and home. Now, my anchor is in Europe: on a continent I've never seen. . . . Now, I'll never think of turning back."

He made the flight in thirty-three and a half hours and immediately became a reluctant folk hero on both sides of the Atlantic. His daughter Reeve says, "People still tell me exactly where they were standing when they heard the news of his landing in Paris."

Amelia Earhart was the first woman to fly alone over the Atlantic Ocean. She did it on May 20, 1932, almost exactly five years after the Lindbergh flight. Reaching Europe somewhat off course, she landed in an open field near Londonderry in northern Ireland. She flew several times across the United States and became involved in encouraging the development of commercial aviation. But she hungered for another adventure. "I have a feeling that there is just about one more good flight left in my system and

I hope this trip is it. Anyway when I have finished this job, I mean to give up long-distance 'stunt' flying." Her next stunt was a circumnavigation of the globe.

Flying west to east, she and navigator Fred Noonan began their quest on June 1, 1937. They reached Lae in New Guinea, but then their trail faded. The Coast Guard Cutter *Itasca* heard her final transmission: "We must be on you but cannot see you . . . gas is running low . . ." President Franklin Roosevelt authorized a search for Earhart involving 9 ships and 66 aircraft. Earhart's disappearance has never been solved.

ABOVE: *Wilbur Wright scurries to keep up with his airborne brother Orville, who is piloting the first sustained, controlled flight by a heavier-than-air craft. The two ushered in the Age of Flight near Kitty Hawk, North Carolina, on December 17, 1903.*
NEXT: *The American Clipper, here soaring over San Francisco, carried 44 passengers in the 1930s; it took the cushy plane nearly 17 hours to travel from New York before arriving in San Francisco.*

SOCIAL REFORM

Reining in Capitalism

Mary had a little lamb, And when she saw it sicken, She shipped it off to Packingtown, And now it's labeled chicken.

Terrifying fact underlay a jingle circulating after Upton Sinclair's fictional journey through the Chicago stockyards—*The Jungle*—was published in 1906. The book sickened readers with revelations of rancid beef and tubercular pork destined for dinner tables. Humorist Finley Peter Dunne described Theodore Roosevelt, who denigrated sensational muckraking journalism as being "engaged in a hand-to-hand conflict with a potted ham" and hurling sausages from a White House window.

Largely because of the book, Congress passed the Pure Food and Drug Act and the Meat Inspection Act in 1906. The largest meat packers applauded the measures to restore public confidence—while many smaller competitors were driven out of business.

A socialist, Sinclair had meant to provoke sympathy for the immigrants who toiled and died in slaughterhouses. Only eight of the book's 308 pages described the filth and confusion of the meat processing plant, where men toiled for 17 cents an hour and sometimes fell into the boiling vats, becoming part of Durham's Pure Leaf Lard. "I aimed at the public's heart," he wrote, "and by accident I hit it in the stomach."

Meatpacking was not the only industry to come under scrutiny. "Prosperity never before imagined, power never yet wielded by man, speed never reached by anything but a meteor, had

made the world irritable, nervous, querulous, unreasonable and afraid." Historian Henry Adams, descendant of two Presidents, vented the doubts of a nation. Industry had nurtured American trade and naval vigor but at great cost: cities darkened by poverty and political scandal as well as by smoke; colossal trusts that menaced cherished notions of fair play.

Children often labored in so-called "sweatshops." The term came from England, where as early as 1850 the word "sweater" described an employer or middleman who exacted monotonous work for very low wages. Sweatshops became widespread in the U.S. during the 1880s, when emigrants from eastern and southern Europe provided a large source of cheap labor. Sometimes they were in the home, where a family might contract to do piecework for pay and everyone pitched in. In addition to garments, they might be involved in shoe manufacture, soap making, cigar making, and the pasting together of artificial flowers. Sweatshops tended to be worse in large cities, where they could be hidden away in slum areas.

In 1911 there were more than 15,000 boys under the age of 16 working in Pennsylvania coal mines. At least two million children under the age of 15 were at work nationwide. Journalist Edwin Markham visited a cigarette factory: "One face followed me still, the gaunt face of a boy . . . pasting tiny labels on the margins of cigarette boxes. All day long he

stuck little oblongs of paper marked with the runic words: 'Cork tips,' 'Cork tips,' 'Cork tips.' That was his message to the world. His pay was 25 cents a thousand and he sat there

---

FROM *THE JUNGLE*

The line of the buildings stood clear-cut and black against the sky; here and there out of the mass rose the great chimneys, with the river of smoke streaming away to the end of the world. It was a study in colours now, this smoke; in the sunset light it was black and brown and grey and purple. All the sordid questions of the place were gone—in the twilight it was a vision of power. To the two who stood watching while the darkness swallowed it up, it seemed a dream of wonder, with its tale of human energy, of things being done, of employment for thousands upon thousands of men, of opportunity and freedom, of life and love and joy. When they came away, arm in arm, Jurgis was saying, "Tomorrow I shall go there and get a job!"

–Upton Sinclair

---

growing bent and haggard, and spending all his energies to promulgate to humanity this news about cork tips."

In 1916 Congress forbade employment of children under 14 in firms engaged in interstate commerce. This legislation was ruled unconstitutional in 1918. Congress imposed an extra 10 percent tax on factories employing young children, which, too, was thrown out. It wasn't until the Fair Labor Standards Act of 1938 that the minimum age was set at 14 for employment outside of school hours in nonmanufacturing jobs; at 16 for employment during school hours in interstate commerce; and at 18 for occupations called hazardous by the secretary of labor.

ABOVE: *Grimy boys, already gainfully employed while still in their adolescence, emerge from a coal mine somewhere in the eastern U.S. around 1910.*

OPPOSITE: *Upton Sinclair as he appeared in his youth. The American author wrote more than 90 books, including* The Jungle *in 1906.*

The AUTOMOBILE

Hitting the Road

By 1895 Detroit was a growing industrial city, noted for steam and gas engines, stoves, and carriages. Entrepreneurs such as Ford, Durant, Leland, Olds, and the Dodge brothers quickly made it the auto capital of the country. In 1986 Michigan retained more auto-manufacturing facilities—114—than any other state and produced 30 percent of the cars made in the U.S. Ohio followed with 51; then Indiana, with 26.

Motor vehicle assembly and parts plants nearly doubled in number between 1909 and 1927, when 1,373 were operating. After 1914 New York and Michigan lost plants to surrounding states. Competition, meanwhile, winnowed automobile firms, many of them former carriage or bicycle makers, from about 250 to 40.

By the 1920s Americans were growing tired of Henry Ford's black Model T, which had dominated the market since 1908. They were excited by new innovations like the electric starter, introduced in 1912. Closed cars and better roads had encouraged driving all year round. Motorists wanted more than just basic transportation.

As head of General Motors, Alfred Sloan was ready to give it to them. GM was in business "to make money, not just to make motor cars," and

Sloan widened the product line, targeting models for sale to different classes of buyers, on the company's installment plan if possible. In the 1920s GM developed its most important strategy, the annual model change. Sloan later said: "The 'laws' of the Paris dressmakers have come to be a factor in the automobile industry .... The changes in the new model should be so novel and attractive as to create ... dissatisfaction with past models."

After World War I the so-called Big Three rose to dominate the automobile industry; in the U.S., Ford dominated with the Model T. In 1921, GM was plunged into financial crisis, but Sloan, who became president in 1923, introduced manufacturing innovations that made GM the unchallenged leader. Among other things, he gave the company a staff-and-line organization that featured autonomous manufacturing divisions, which facilitated management and became the model of other companies.

The third of the Big Three—Chrysler—was formed when the Maxwell Motor Company failed and Walter P. Chrysler was hired to reorganize it. It became the Chrysler Corporation in 1925 and grew enormously with the acquisition of the Dodge Brothers company in 1928. When Ford had to halt production for 18 months to switch from the Model T to the Model A, Chrysler broke into the low-priced market with the Plymouth.

By 1929 the Big Three were supplying three-fourths of the autos sold in the U.S. The five largest independents—Hudson, Nash, Packard, Studebaker, and Willys-Overland—produced most of the rest. But there were dozens of other manufacturers, most of whom were wiped out during the Great Depression of the 1930s. The Depression also reduced the number of cars sold: Production declined from a peak of more than five million in 1929 to a low of just over a million in 1932. Production had still not reached the 1929 level when World War II broke out.

The invention of the car not only changed American business, it changed the American landscape. After 1850, railroads handled most of the long-haul transport. America's roads were left largely neglected. But the automobile's arrival increased demand for good roads.

City streets were improving in 1900, but rural roads were mostly unimproved dirt tracks. By 1904 only 144 miles of rural roads had any type of pavement. Service stations and road maps were as rare as pavement, so motorists had to be both mechanics and navigators when they were

ROUTE 66

Designated officially in 1926, Route 66 ran diagonally across the West from Chicago to Los Angeles, linking hundreds of predominantly rural communities. John Steinbeck called it the "Mother Road" in *The Grapes of Wrath* and sent his Oakies hopefully along it. During the Great Depression thousands found work on it, and it was reported "continuously paved" in 1938. Garages and diners sprang up along its length; motels evolved from the earlier tourist homes and auto camps. The route served its travelers well until the Interstate Highway System came along; the final section of the original was replaced by Interstate 40 at Williams, Arizona, in October 1984.

Among the postwar tourists who traveled Route 66 was Robert William Troup, Jr., of Harrisburg, Pennsylvania. Bobby was a former pianist with the Tommy Dorsey band and an ex-marine captain. In 1946, Bobby wrote a song about the highway:

If you ever plan to motor west:
Travel my way, the highway that's the best.
Get your kicks on Route 66!
It winds from Chicago to L.A.,
More than 2,000 miles all the way,
Get your kicks on Route 66!
Now you go through St. Looey, Joplin, Missouri!
And Oklahoma City looks mighty pretty.
You'll see Amarillo, Gallup, New Mexico,
Flagstaff ... Barstow, San Bernardino.
Won't you get hip to this timely tip:
When you make that California trip,
Get your kicks on Route 66! ∎

OPPOSITE: *Innovations in mass production introduced by Henry Ford quickly spread throughout the industry, evidenced by these cars nearing completion at the Packard Motor Company in Michigan.*

on the road. With each year, however, the number of cars shot upward (from 8,000 in 1900 to 9.2 million in 1920), and road builders struggled to meet the growing demand. State and local governments improved thousands of miles annually and began receiving federal aid with a $500,000 appropriation from the government in 1912.

The U.S. had more than three million miles of roads in 1920, but good ones were still exceptions. Only 35,000 miles of rural roads had been paved. Routes linking regions, such as the transcontinental Lincoln Highway, were privately funded. Road improvement and new construction averaged tens of thousands of miles each year.

The first coherent system of federally funded roads was authorized in 1921; a grid of national highways was set in 1924; and uniform signs were adopted in 1925. High-speed divided highways with controlled access were adapted from European models. In 1940 the first 160 miles of the Pennsylvania Turnpike opened.

By 1950, federal funds had built a basic network of 644,000 miles of highways. An additional 1.6 million miles of state and local roads had been surfaced with gravel or paved since 1920. Despite the progress, many new roads were outdated in design or overcrowded. Impressed by the German Autobahn, Gen. Dwight David Eisenhower recalled, "During World War II, I saw the superlative system of German national highways crossing that country and offering the possibility . . . to drive with speed and safety at the same time." On June 29, 1956, Eisenhower, now President, signed the authorizing act for 41,000 miles of quality highways to link the nation. The mileage was later lengthened to 44,000 miles and intended to connect 90 percent of all cities of 50,000 people. The highways allowed a coast-to-coast drive without seeing a traffic light.

RIGHT: *The Model T Ford brought opportunity for change. Here, a South Dakota man and his family leave drought-stricken lands for a brand-new beginning in the Pacific Northwest.*

WORLD WAR ONE

Into the Trenches

When the guns of August sounded in 1914, they heralded a war that would engulf the world for four years and kill nearly 15 million people.

The action of one man lit the fuse: On June 28, 1914, a Serbian nationalist assassinated Archduke Franz Ferdinand, the heir to Austria-Hungary's throne, in the city of Sarajevo. Austria-Hungary, backed by Germany, threatened to declare war on Serbia. Russia came to Serbia's defense. These entangling alliances caused the great powers to tumble almost inadvertently into a war that pitted the Central Powers—mainly Germany, Austria-Hungary, and Turkey—against the Allies—mainly France, Great Britain, Russia, Italy, Japan, and, after 1917, the United States.

The Germans attacked across western Europe with more than a million men, fighting across Belgium to the Marne River, near Paris. There the French rallied with the help of the British and drove them back. The two armies dug in, facing each other in a double line of trenches 400 miles long. They devoted nearly four years to bloody attacks and counterattacks across no man's land, inflicting millions of casualties. In the east, a huge Russian army moved against Germany but, after making a few gains against the smaller and better-led Germans, withdrew. Nonetheless, the fighting continued along an ever shifting front from the Baltic Sea to the Black Sea.

In America, President Woodrow Wilson looked across the Atlantic and hoped to keep the U.S. out of it, saying, "God helping me, I will if it is possible." He told the American people, "The

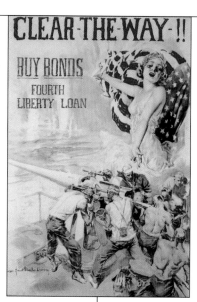

United States must be neutral in fact as well as in name." But neutrality was difficult. The British set up a naval blockade to keep countries from trading with Germany, who responded by using submarines to sink enemy merchant ships found in the waters around Britain. When a German torpedo sank the British passenger ship *Lusitania* in May 1915, nearly 1,200 people, including 128 Americans, were killed. The American populace was enraged. Wilson warned Germany that if it sank any American ships, it would risk war with the U.S. Germany backed down.

In 1916, with the war in its third futile year, the people of Germany and Austria were on the verge of starvation, cut off from supplies by British ships. Risking U.S. intervention, the Germans resumed the submarine attacks and hoped to defeat Britain and France before the Americans became involved.

On March 1, 1917, the British intercepted a telegram from Germany promising the Mexican government the return of Texas, New Mexico, and Arizona if Mexico would join the German side against the United States. American anger at Germany increased. Two weeks later the Russian people, wearied with hunger, ineffectual leadership, and unending bloodshed, rose up and swept away its monarchy and Nicholas II, the tsar of Russia. It seemed likely that Russia's war effort would soon collapse.

Just three days after the tsar's fall, German submarines sank three American merchant ships, leading the U.S. Congress to declare war against

the Germans. Wilson had hoped he could build an army of volunteers in America, but three weeks after the declaration of war only 32,000 men had volunteered, not nearly enough. The Selective Service Act was passed and an intense public relations campaign enacted to thwart any public opposition; draftees were made into heroes by parades and patriotic festivals. Men between the ages of 21 and 30 were required to register as of June 5, 1917, and nearly 10 million did.

Despite fears that African Americans would resist the draft, 400,000 served among the 3.7 million American troops in France. They were mostly used as longshoremen, supply troops, orderlies, and musicians. Discrimination kept their ranks below captain, but New York's 369th Infantry, the Harlem Hellfighters, won more than 150 Croix de Guerre decorations and were honored with parades at home in New York City.

The buildup accelerated throughout 1918, with more than a million Americans engaged in combat by the end of the year. But America had no Air Force squadrons in 1917 and only eight in May 1918, all equipped with French airplanes. The government made the mistake of trying to design new planes and guns instead of adapting British and French weapons already being manufactured by American factories. Artillery, planes, and machine guns all had to be bought or borrowed from the French.

Meanwhile, amid growing unrest in Russia, a group of Bolshevik, or Communist, revolutionaries led by V. I. Lenin took control of the government. The new government, eager for peace, quickly acquiesced to German demands and withdrew from the war, which allowed Germany to move thousands of troops from the eastern front to the west against the French and British.

ABOVE: *Red Cross workers, fleeing a German bombardment, scramble to move orphans into a sandbagged bunker in Belgium during World War One.*
OPPOSITE: *Patriotic advertisements for "Liberty Loans" sought to raise money for the U.S. armed forces from noncombatants at home.*

But by the spring of 1918 troop ships were delivering nearly 100,000 American soldiers a month across the Atlantic to help the Allies. They reached the battlefields of France in time to help block the last great German offensive in early June 1918. Germany's government collapsed, and Kaiser Wilhelm, the German ruler, went into exile.

In January 1918 President Wilson had delivered a speech, the "Fourteen Points," that summed up his vision for a postwar settlement. In it, Wilson advocated free trade, democracy, open agreements, and the formation of "a general association of nations." The speech was reprinted in 60 million pamphlets distributed all over the world, including behind enemy lines. Wilson's plan was just, which convinced the German leadership to accept a peace offer from the Allies, and all fighting ended at 11 a.m. on November 11, 1918.

In December 1918 President Wilson journeyed to Paris to help the Allies prepare a peace treaty that he hoped would lead to limits on arms, fairer colonial policies, and a League of Nations—an assembly where all member countries could meet regularly to discuss how to settle quarrels without going to war. When the President arrived in Paris with his wife Edith, he was greeted as a hero: "Paris," Mrs. Wilson wrote, "was wild with celebration. Every inch was covered with cheering."

Despite Wilson's promise of a just peace, the treaty signed at the Versailles Palace on June 28 forced Germany to give back a large territory it had taken from France 48 years earlier, as well as lands to the east. It was forced to disband most of its armed forces, admit that Germany alone was to blame for starting the war, and pay billions of dollars in reparations. The harsh terms embittered the defeated Germans even more and planted the seeds of another and even bloodier conflict to come.

LEFT: *An American gun crew inches forward during heavy fighting in the Meuse-Argonne offensive in France in the autumn of 1918. Nearly 120,000 Americans fell in this costly battle.*

WOMEN GO
to the POLLS

Fighting for Votes

"Taxation without representation is tyranny," declared some proponents of votes for women. "Give women suffrage," claimed others, "and all wars will cease." Local campaigns supplemented pickets at the White House, hunger strikes, and even imprisonment.

Between 1893 and 1908, according to scholar Nell Irvin Painter, suffragists waged 480 separate campaigns just to get the issue of suffrage on state ballots and succeeded only 17 times. Of these only three passed—Colorado (1893) and Idaho and Utah (1896).

By 1910 females composed more than one-fifth of the nation's work force. Women increasingly demanded political liberation to match their newfound financial independence. They shared the vote with men in 11 states by 1914 (Wyoming was the first state to grant the vote, in 1869) but nationwide suffrage seemed a distant goal. Advocates wanted a constitutional amendment; male lawmakers sidestepped the issue in Congress, claiming the states should decide.

In the first decade of the 20th century, a solidarity movement began among American women. They began calling themselves feminists around 1912, but some, including, surprisingly, Eleanor Roosevelt, initially opposed female suffrage, arguing that women could do more good working in the social organizations they formed.

Florence Kelley, daughter of a Pennsylvania congressman and close friend of Susan B.

Anthony, combined passion for social justice with a firm belief in the power of facts. She stormed into the sweatshops and tenements of Chicago to see for herself how women and children were being exploited. In New York in 1899 she became general secretary of the new National Consumers' League and organized boycotts of products from rogue employers. She helped develop a model statute of minimum wage laws, which were enacted in 13 states and the District of Columbia. Jane Addams (1860–1935) worked from her base in her community house in the slums of Chicago, striving to reform factory hours, sanitation, and health care. At the 1912 convention of the Progressive Party, the only major party to support women's suffrage, she seconded the nomination of Teddy Roosevelt.

Alice Paul learned militant tactics in the votes-for-women campaign in London and brought them back to America. By age 23 she had been in prison three times. She and her group picketed the White House, drawing attention to the hypocrisy of President Wilson, who fought for worldwide democracy but would not extend it to American women.

The major roles played by women during World War I did much to break down the final resistance to women's suffrage. Amendments to the Constitution giving women the vote had been introduced into Congress in 1878 and 1914, but

SUSAN B. ANTHONY

Susan Anthony, severe in her gold spectacles, black dress and tight austere bob of hair, is the stereotype of the "old maid" reformer of the Gilded Age. She was, in fact, tough, canny, funny in private, difficult to shock and pungent in her rhetoric: "Women," she said, "we might as well be great Newfoundland dogs baying to the moon as to be petitioning for the passage of bills without the power to vote." And again, "For a woman to marry a man for support is a demoralizing condition. And for a man to marry a woman merely because she has a beautiful figure is a degradation." Nor have all the issues she and nineteenth- and early-twentieth-century feminists fought gone away in a hundred years. Argument has hardly ceased over a woman's right to control her reproduction, equality in the workplace, political and legal status or the right, even, to dress as she likes.

—Harold Evans, 1998

both were soundly defeated. By 1918, just after the war, both major political parties were committed to women's suffrage. The amendment was carried by the necessary two-thirds majorities in both the House and the Senate in May 1919 and June 1919, respectively.

On August 18, 1920, women gained the right to vote with ratification of the 19th Amendment to the Constitution. "The right of citizens of the United States to vote shall not be denied or abridged by the United States or by any State on account of sex."

ABOVE: *A large group of women wearing "Votes for Women" banners fill the office and surround the desk of Kentucky Governor Edwin P. Morrow as he signs the Anthony Amendment, making Kentucky the 24th state to ratify giving women the vote.*

OPPOSITE: *Proud suffragettes pose on a rooftop with the American flag to celebrate their securing the right to vote.*

GOING DRY

Prohibition and Repeal

Bessie Laythe Scovell, president, addressed the annual convention of the WCTU, the Woman's Christian Temperance Union, in Mankato, Minnesota, at the end of the 19th century.

"Today we are met to execute plans (not Indians) to carry on our peaceful war for 'God and Home and Native Land.' There is an enemy in the land more stealthy than the Indian, more deadly in its work—the alcoholic liquor traffic. It is killing thousands annually and destroying hun-

dreds of homes. We toil and sacrifice today to hasten the tomorrow when this enemy will be executed upon the gibbet of public opinion."

In the U.S. an alcoholic beverage was defined as any drink with more than 0.5 percent alcohol. Beer had 3 to 8 percent, wine 10 to 20. The move to ban its manufacture and sale arose during a period of strong religious revivalism in the 1820s and 1830s. Saloons and bars were thought to be destructive of family life and factory discipline.

Prostitutes hung out in them, wages were gambled away, and ward bosses visited to buy votes on election day.

The first prohibition law was passed in Maine in 1846, and a number of state legislatures followed suit before the Civil War. By January 1920 prohibition was already in effect in 33 states. The 18th Amendment to the Constitution went into effect on January 17, 1920.

Prohibition was unpopular and not very firmly enforced. Police were easily bribed to overlook the beer that was still being brewed, and one federal agent, Izzy Einstein, reported that in most American cities it took just half an hour to find alcohol. In Chicago, he said, it took 21 minutes, Atlanta 17, Pittsburgh 11—and in New Orleans the search occupied just 35 seconds! (His taxi driver provided it.) Bootleggers imported much of their illegal bounty from Canada and shipped in the rest. Ships carrying liquor anchored just outside New York's jurisdiction, and bootleggers used their ingenuity to get it ashore. Some liquor, according to historian Harold Evans, "came in as fruit, some was flown in and dropped in lakes, some was fired ashore in torpedoes."

Illicit bars called speakeasies screened their clientele at the door and hid their liquor from the occasional raid by police. New York's "21" on 52nd Street still displayed, in 1996, a cellar stacked with bottles hidden behind a brick wall that slid aside at the touch of a secret button.

On December 5, 1933, Utah provided the two-thirds majority needed when it voted for the 21st Amendment to the Constitution—which repealed the 18th, Prohibition. It was the first, and so far the only, time a constitutional amendment has been repealed. After the repeal of Prohibition, several states continued independently to ban liquor, but by 1966 all had bowed to the inevitable.

Prohibition was not a complete failure. Public drunkenness virtually disappeared, and while some people died or went blind from bad moonshine, diseases and deaths from alcohol declined. The head of the Hudson Guild in New York said, "A great number of men who always stopped in at

F. SCOTT FITZGERALD

They were careless people, Tom and Daisy—they smashed up things and creatures and then retreated back into their money or their vast carelessness, or whatever it was that kept them together, and let other people clean up the mess they had made." In *The Great Gatsby*, F. Scott Fitzgerald wrote of the love and death of a wealthy bootlegger, as told by a curious young cousin who was a spectator.

Young, handsome, and socially privileged, Fitzgerald acted out the legend of "the sad young men" who made up Gertrude Stein's "lost generation." Disillusioned youths who flouted traditions and taboos cherished by their parents, they and their girls were the flappers of the Jazz Age. "The very rich are different from you and me," he wrote. "They possess and enjoy early and it does something to them, makes them soft where we are hard, and cynical where we are trustful in a way that, unless you were born rich, it is very difficult to understand. They think, deep in their hearts, that they are better than we are." Fitzgerald and his troubled wife Zelda threw themselves into having fun— "I had everything I wanted and knew I would never be so happy again."

But beneath the fun-filled surface a poignancy emerged. Fitzgerald ended *Gatsby* "So we beat on, boats against the current, borne back ceaselessly into the past." ■

the saloon on the way home and almost emptied their pay packets now bring their wages home. They and their families are living more peaceably than they did before."

But Prohibition spawned the organized crime families that still exist. Chicagoan John Torrio, the father of modern American gangsterism, made bootlegging a multimillion-dollar business by doing deals with the big brewers, bribing the police and politicians, and getting the Chicago gangs to agree to divide up the bootlegging turf.

OPPOSITE: *During the height of Prohibition, liquor is spilled out into the sewer as New York City Deputy Police Commissioner John A. Leach personally supervises.*

PICTURES *That* TALK

Movies in America

Americans have had a long love affair with movies. From fumbling beginnings around the turn of the 20th century, movies evolved from "peep shows" to complex, full-length spectacles shown in luxurious movie palaces that seated thousands. By early in the 1920s movies had become America's fifth most lucrative industry. During an average week in 1938, when the country was still struggling to shake loose from the Great Depression, America's population of 130 million people bought 80 million movie tickets. Life on the silver screen was richer, fuller, more exciting, and a way to escape the travails of everyday life.

By 1916, the fledging industry had fully resettled from New York to an obscure section of Los Angeles called Hollywood, where the sun was more reliable and the temperatures conducive to working outside, all year round. There the first moguls invented the modern studio system. They saw the new medium's potential—a rich but inexpensive source of entertainment for working-class Americans. They founded studios that controlled stables of producers, directors, writers, and stars. Films got longer and better.

Hollywood's first studio was built on a lot on Sunset Boulevard a few years later, and soon some 20 companies were filming in the area. Cecil B. DeMille, Jesse Lasky, and Samuel Goldwyn made *The Squaw Man* in 1914 in a barn just a block from today's Hollywood and Vine.

Producers at first tried to keep actors anonymous, fearing that if they got to be famous they would ask for more money. And did they ever!

Mary Pickford, who could convincingly play a 10-year-old when she was in her late 20s, was a shrewd and iron-willed negotiator, and by 1915 she had negotiated her pay to $10,000 a week. Charlie Chaplin and Douglas Fairbanks were soon at the same level, and in 1919, to head off a salary squeeze by the studios, the three banded together with director D. W. Griffith to form their own company, United Artists. Said one executive: "The lunatics have taken charge of the asylum."

Stars powered the system. Britain's Lord Louis Mountbattan said of Mary Pickford and Douglas Fairbanks: They were "treated like royalty, and in fact they behaved in the same sort of dignified way that royalty did." When the first great "Latin lover," Rudolph Valentino, died in 1926 of peritonitis, 30,000 fans swarmed his funeral. There were reports that at least a dozen overwrought fans committed suicide.

When the movies learned to talk, much changed. Stars with thick European accents disappeared and trained Broadway actors took over. Directors emerged as the new stars, with men like Alfred Hitchcock, Cecil B. DeMille, and Otto Preminger choosing the cast for their films, hiring technicians, coaching the actors, making decisions about lighting and camera angles and the final editing. Movie magazines fed fans' desire to know everything about their favorite stars, and the studio publicity machines cranked out features that made their stars seem like ordinary people, on the one hand, and exotic creatures of wealth and luxury on the other.

CLARA BOW

Clara Bow's beauty made her a silent-era star, but her voice killed her career. She was born poor in Brooklyn in 1905. In high school she won a beauty contest and set out for Hollywood. A small part in *Beyond the Rainbow* in 1922 brought her to the attention of producers, and she was soon featured in silent films like *Mantrap* and *Dancing Mothers*. She became the country's "It Girl" in 1927 when she starred in the film of Elinor Glyn's novel It. With bobbed hair and big eyes, she came to personify the public's idea of the sexy, free-living flapper of the 1920s.

She was living a wild life to match her image, and when scandals broke, her career suffered. And when "talkies" came along and fans heard her thick Brooklyn accent, it ended. She moved to a cattle ranch in Nevada with her husband, former Western star Rex Bell, and lived there peacefully until her death in 1965. ■

Spectacular features from directors like Victor Flemming crowded the screen with "casts of thousands." Well-known authors—F. Scott Fitzgerald, Aldous Huxley, William Faulkner—took jobs writing screenplays for large sums of money. Comics like the Marx Brothers inspired mayhem on the screen, and "screwball" comedies included, in 1938, Howard Hawks's *Bringing Up Baby* with Cary Grant and Katharine Hepburn. Musicals, war movies, gangland pictures, mysteries, Westerns, and horror films all attracted moviegoers seeking escape from everyday life.

OPPOSITE: *Clara Bow was the original "It Girl" and one of the first stars of the silent screen.*
ABOVE: *Moviegoers flock to see* City Lights, *the latest Charlie Chaplin film, around 1931.*
NEXT: Gone With the Wind, *released in 1939, was an epic smash for Hollywood. When adjusted for inflation, it remains one of the highest grossing movies ever produced.*

DAVID O. SELZNICK'S
"GONE WITH THE WIND"
in TECHNICOLOR

WAVES *of* NEW AMERICANS

Immigration to the States

Immigration patterns have strongly reflected changes in U.S. policy. Record keeping began in 1820, when ships' masters were required to report arriving alien passengers. Great numbers of Irish and Germans came in the mid-19th century. The designation "immigrant" was first made in 1868. Only "paupers, vagabonds and possible convicts" were excluded until the immigration ban on Chinese in 1882. Minimum health qualifications were set in the 1890s.

The principal immigration reception center in the U.S. was a small island off the southwestern tip of Manhattan named for merchant Samuel Ellis, who owned it in the 1770s. Between 1892 and 1954, 17 million immigrants entered the U.S. through its portals. First was a 15-year-old Irish girl named Annie Moore, who was at the head of the line when the facility opened on January 1, 1892. Her two brothers were right behind her.

American attitudes toward immigration were, at best, ambivalent. Published in *The Atlantic Monthly* in 1892, Thomas Bailey Aldrich's poem "The Unguarded Gates," exemplified this sentiment: "Wide open and unguarded stand our gates, / And through them presses a wild motley throng." Inspectors at the recently opened entry facilities at Ellis Island in New York Harbor were scrutinizing new arrivals as they never had before. Millions of immigrants were not so much welcomed to the country as asked to prove their worthiness to enter.

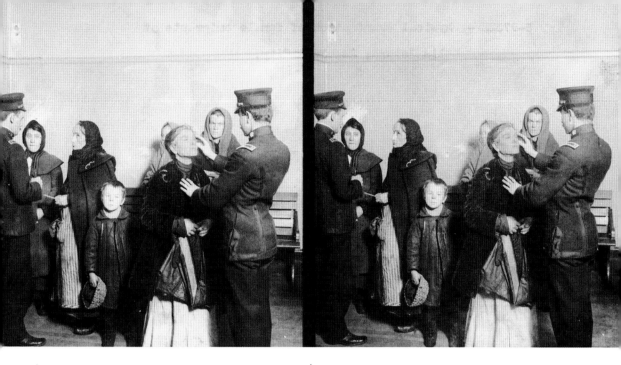

Of the 17 million immigrants who were processed at Ellis Island, five million were first- and second-class passengers. They were not required to undergo the rigorous inspection process on Ellis Island but were given a cursory inspection aboard ship, then passed through. The government theorized that these wealthier passengers were less likely than their poorer brethren to become public charges due to illnesses or legal problems. Only steerage and third-class passengers were sent through Ellis Island, where they underwent a medical and legal inspection.

Doctors would scan every immigrant that came off the ship for obvious physical ailments and by 1916 had become adept at conducting "six second physicals." In those few seconds, they boasted they could spot various medical conditions—anemia, tuberculosis, varicose veins, "feeble-mindedness," rickets—that would bar an immigrant from entry. Only about two percent were excluded, most because the inspector decided to exclude the immigrant, a heartbreaking situation to have come so far only to be turned away at the last minute.

New York City handled the lion's share—75 percent—of the 26 million immigrants who entered from 1870 to 1920. In the busiest decade, 1900 to 1909, nine million people arrived. On the West Coast, between 1910 and 1940, about one million immigrants entered the United States via the Angel Island Immigration Station. Located on the largest island in San Francisco Bay, the station was set up to facilitate implementation of the Chinese Exclusion Act of 1882. The facility provided a place to detain immigrants while considering their applications to enter the country. In addition to China, immigrants here came from Japan, Russia, India, Korea, the Philippines, Australia, and New Zealand

Numbers from northern Europe were at an apogee, from southern and eastern Europe still rising. A person's point of entry into the United States yielded very different experiences: The facilities that greeted immigrants ranged from federal efficiency at Ellis Island to laxness at New Orleans. Ports competed for the transoceanic traffic—and made sure that not too many immigrants lingered; railroads ran right onto wharves. The first American soil an immigrant touched might be in St. Louis.

OPPOSITE: *In the early 1900s, groups of immigrants walked across a pier on Ellis Island as they took their first steps to entering the United States.*

ABOVE: *Rigorous physical exams were the norm for new arrivals to make sure they were in good health. In this stereoscopic image of Ellis Island, a physician gives a check-up to a newly arrived woman in 1911.*

Norwegians, Swedes, and Danes (in that order by total immigrants) arrived in great numbers after the American Civil War, forced out of their homelands by exploding populations and a shortage of good farmland. Norway was second to Ireland in the loss of its 19th-century population to the United States. Scandinavians, many of them farmers, lumbermen, and miners, settled mainly in the upper Midwest. Later many went to the Pacific Coast in search of land and jobs. "This is just like Norway!" wrote one Norwegian, describing Washington State's Puget Sound area.

Beyond the "arched gateway" of New York's harbor lay work in the industrial boomtowns extending west to the Mississippi River. By 1920 the northern states east of the river, taken together with the West Coast, held 91 percent of the foreign-born population. Many English immigrants settled in Utah; by 1890 one out of seven residents of Salt Lake City was English. Immigrants held majorities in many major cities, though they were being gained on by native-born

Americans—and by their own children—everywhere but in the southern New England states.

Seventy-five percent of immigrants settled in the cities of a nation that was 50 percent rural. Though no group formed a majority in any major city, Jews and Italians had a plurality in New York and Philadelphia, Polish in Chicago and Cleveland, Germans in Pittsburgh and Milwaukee, Irish in Boston and San Francisco. Factory owners found cheap, tractable labor among the recent arrivals, replacing Germans and Irish with Eastern Europeans. One Pittsburgh mill owner advertised, "Syrians, Poles, and Romanians preferred."

Analyzing patterns of immigration reveals interesting trends. Chain migration—the tendency to follow in the footsteps of friends and relatives—gave ports different ethnic character. Large numbers of Irish immigrants settled in Boston. Many Germans followed relatives to Baltimore, Maryland, while Italians favored New York and Philadelphia. Gulf of Mexico ports drew on Cuba and the Caribbean rim. The West Coast extended an ambivalent welcome across the Pacific. Chinese laborers surged into San Francisco until their exclusion in 1882. From 1900 to 1909, 139,712 Japanese came to the U.S., half of them to Honolulu. In 1920, 43 percent of Hawaii's population was Japanese.

The great wave of immigration peaked at the turn of the 19th century. Two kinds of immigration patterns emerged, consisting of those who "pulled" and those "pushed." The pulled followed economic incentives and often came alone to the United States, later returning to their country of origin or using their savings to bring members of their family to their new country. Italian populations tend to follow this pattern. Four million Italians arrived by 1920. Most were males, intending to return to Italy, and almost half did. Greeks, Romanians, and Serbs returned in even greater percentages. Among those "pushed" were three million Jews driven from Russia by edict and pogrom.

There was money in immigrants, and promoters of states, railroads, and steamship lines fanned the flames of "America fever." A Minnesota pamphlet cajoled, "Exchange the tyrannies and thankless toil of the old world for the freedom and independence of the new."

But such massive waves of new immigrants, most of them farmers, led to exploitation. In cities, hundreds of poor families were crammed in tenements, living in tiny dark rooms lacking windows or any means of sanitation. Men and women worked long hours in factories with dangerous work conditions. Seamstresses worked in sweatshops that became notorious on March 25, 1911, when a fire broke out at the Triangle Shirtwaist Company, killing 146 laborers. Despite poor living conditions and harsh working conditions, some immigrants who came to the United States found better financial opportunities. British workers sought higher pay in the U.S. factories, while Canadians fled economic depression.

After the flood of immigrants into the country had reached a peak, legislation was introduced to limit their numbers. Quota Laws were passed beginning in 1921, followed by the Immigration Act and the National Origins Act in 1924. These attempted both to slow immigration and to control its character: Quotas of immigrants allowed in were based on a percentage of the number of an ethnic group already here. The ethnic flavor of the "old immigrants" was protected, favoring those from Northern Europe and curtailing numbers from southeastern Europe. Besides adopting a system of quotas based on national origin and excluding many Asians, the acts also set an annual ceiling on immigration.

In 1924 ethnic quotas all but closed the gates on eastern and southern Europe. Only after World War II would the United States welcome refugees by the hundreds of thousands from war-torn Europe. The quota system was officially done away with in 1965 in a favor of a new one, based on a "first come, first served" policy.

THE NEW COLOSSUS

On a Plaque at the Statue of Liberty:
Not like the brazen giant of Greek fame,
With conquering limbs astride from land to land;
Here at our sea-washed, sunset gates shall stand
A mighty woman with a torch, whose flame
Is the imprisoned lightning, and her name
Mother of Exiles. From her beacon-hand
Glows world-wide welcome; her mild eyes command
the air-bridged harbor that twin cities frame.
"Keep ancient lands, your storied pomp!" cries she
With silent lips. "Give me your tired, your poor,
Your huddled masses yearning to breathe free,
The wretched refuse of your teeming shore.
Send these, the homeless, tempest-tost to me,
I lift my lamp beside the golden door!"

—Emma Lazarus

OPPOSITE: *Drying laundry hangs from the windows of the tenements lining Elizabeth Street in New York City in 1912. Living conditions for new immigrants were often poor, cramped, and often unsanitary.*

RIDING *the* AIRWAVES

Radio Reaches America

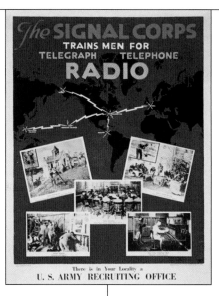

U.S. Patents 841,387 and 879,532 went to Lee de Forest. In 1907 his Audion vacuum tube used electric power to amplify electromagnetic waves, an important step in transmitting the human voice. De Forest installed the first radiophones on U.S. Navy vessels. Radios used vacuum tubes, which could be replaced separately, until smaller, cheaper, and more durable transistors took over in the 1960s.

Originally made as hobby items, radios started appearing in stores in 1920. Even though a good radio soon cost almost $100, by 1924 Americans had bought 2.5 million of them. Radio commercials began in August 1922; ten minutes on WEAF (later WNBC) cost $100. Sponsors underwrote many popular programs. The first regular licensed broadcasting began on August 20 of that year.

Radio brought rural families closer to news and weather reports in the 1920s and 1930s. Radio networks used program circuits, AT&T lines akin to telephone wires. Only 583 stations—all AM (Amplitude Modulation)—were operating in 1934. To cut down on interference, regulations reduced the number of stations broadcasting at night by half. On December 6, 1923, President Calvin Coolidge addressed Congress and for the first time a presidential address was broadcast.

The first U.S. President to recognize the enormous power that radio gave him—to enter America's living rooms and address the people directly—was Franklin Delano Roosevelt. He gave scores of "fireside chats" during his years in office, the first on Sunday night, March 12, 1933,

the day before the country's reorganized banks, which had been closed a few days before for a four-day "bank holiday," were to reopen. An estimated 60 million hung on his every word as he explained the banking system in friendly tones and with thoroughness and candor. The next day confidence was restored when the banks reopened. FDR used fireside chats effectively to belittle critics, explain complex issues, and rally the American people to policies.

But mostly radio meant entertainment. Music of all sorts came across the airwaves. Big bands broadcast from dance halls to every corner of the country. Guy Lombardo and his Royal Canadians became a New Year's Eve fixture. On Christmas Day, 1931, the Metropolitan Opera began its long run of Saturday afternoon broadcasts. In 1937 NBC began a program with Maestro Arturo Toscanini: For 18 years he and his orchestra performed classic symphonic and operatic repertoires on the air. Recordings of broadcasts are still available. In 1941 Martin Block became the first disc jockey, on "The Make Believe Ballroom." He played recordings while describing a hall with bands and singers.

In 1939 broadcasters were devoting just 7 percent of airtime to news, but that increased to 20 percent by 1944. Still, music was by far the dominant programming. Twenty million American homes owned a radio in 1934, 30 million in 1942, and in 1950 some 40 million.

Radio dramas also captured large audiences. Orson Welles's October 30, 1938, dramatization

This . . . is London," intoned Edward R. Murrow nightly, from his posting in Europe. Millions imitated his preamble, allowing a second of hesitation between the first word and the second. He grew up in the Northwest and came to New York to work for CBS in 1935. Two years later Murrow was posted to Europe, just in time for World War II. His first broadcast was from Vienna in 1938, where he reported the Anschluss, Austria's capitulation to Germany. During the war he broadcast regularly from Europe, keeping Americans up-to-date on the progress of the war and on the battering the city of London was taking during the Blitz in 1940. Listeners could even hear the sounds of sirens, anti-aircraft fire, and real bombs falling. By 1943 his was the principal voice describing the war to millions of Americans in their living rooms across the country. He saw himself not just as a broadcaster but also as an educator, telling people what they needed to know and providing information they could not acquire on their own. A chain-smoker, his ever-present cigarettes finally killed him in 1965. ■

of *War of the Worlds* revealed radio's capacity to terrify listeners as well as entertain them. Soap operas like "Romance of Helen Trent" began broadcasting in 1933. Mystery dramas came along, too: "The Shadow" in 1930, "Inner Sanctum" in 1941, and "The Whistler" in 1942.

The Federal Communications Commission approved stereo broadcasting early in the 1960s, and FM (Frequency Modulation), with better sound quality, gained fans among music lovers. The AM spectrum was full in most major markets by 1962, and new stations, especially in suburban areas, turned to FM. After two decades of rapid growth, FM in 1977 was the medium of broadcast on 2,873 commercial and 870 nonprofit stations, up from 960 and 194 in 1962. By the end of the 1970s, FM reached a larger audience than AM, which nevertheless led in stations and profitability.

OPPOSITE: *This 1920s poster for the U.S. Army advertises training for recruits in the latest technology: radio.*
ABOVE: *Performing for NBC radio in 1937, renowned trumpet player Louis Armstrong conducts his band.*

The STOCK MARKET CRASH

A Roaring Silence

The Gin and Jazz Age, the Dollar Decade, the Roaring Twenties—the era was all of those. Hemlines came up, inhibitions went down. Flappers with bobbed hair danced the night away. A hot sound called jazz caught on. Bands led by the elegant Duke Ellington, Fletcher Henderson, and others played at exotic nightclubs. In New York City's Harlem, the Cotton Club was tops.

After a post-World War I recession, big business started booming in 1922. Steel and automobile manufacturing grew through the decade, but small businesses—more vulnerable to economic swings than large companies—failed by the tens of thousands.

As their wages declined, coal miners, textile workers, and farmers could ill afford new products. But if cash was not available for luxuries, credit was—for radios and vacuum cleaners as well as cars.

Speculation in stocks inflated the value of businesses, and the bubble of false prosperity burst in the crash of 1929. Throughout the late 20s, the stock market had been climbing, fueled by exuberant speculation. After reaching a high in August 1929, share prices began to fall during September and early October, but investors continued to buy. Then on October 18 the market began a dramatic plunge.

On October 24, Black Thursday, six leading Wall Street bankers met at the House of Morgan to work out a way to save the bull market. But by 11:00 a.m. the market had lost $9 billion in value. A reporter described the traders on the floor of the Stock Exchange: "Some stood with feet apart and shoulders hunched forward as though to brace themselves against the gusts of selling orders which drove them about the floor like autumn leaves in a gale."

The Big Six bankers had pooled assets to save the market, and after their meeting Richard Whitney, vice president of the Exchange, bought 10,000 shares of U.S. Steel. Then, still trying to prop up the market, he walked the floor, purchasing 200,000 shares of several stocks for $20 million. Late in the day the market rallied somewhat, and at close was down just $3 billion.

But after a calm weekend, Black Monday loomed. By now the market was so overvalued that no one group of bankers could control it or stop it from falling. And, at the opening bell, fall it did. General Electric dropped 48 points; Eastman Kodak 42; U.S. Steel 18. When the president of National City Bank, Charles Mitchell, was seen to be smiling as he emerged from Morgan's Bank in the afternoon, it was taken to be a hopeful sign; but he had been there to arrange a loan to cover his own losses. The Big Six were quietly selling.

Black Tuesday, October 29, was, according to economist John Kenneth Galbraith, "the most devastating day in the history of the New York stock market and it may have been the most devastating day in the history of markets." By the closing bell, $32 billion had been lost as investors dumped more than 16.4 million shares.

The Great Depression descended upon the United States. A Kansas City insurance salesman named John Schwitzgebel, sitting in his club, dropped the financial page he had been reading and shouted: "Tell the boys I can't pay them what I owe them" and shot himself twice in the chest. Hardest hit were investors who had played the market by putting down 10 percent in cash and borrowing the rest—buying "on margin."

Overnight the American dream became a nightmare. Investors lost as much money on October 29 as the U.S. had spent fighting World War I. By 1932 nearly a third of all American workers were unemployed and national output was cut in half. By 1933 a fourth of all the nation's farmers had lost their land.

Stricken Americans wrote daily to the White House asking for work. The poor grew poorer, while once prosperous families fell victim to bank failures. The Rockefeller family lost four-fifths of its fortune. The Vanderbilt family lost $40 million in railroads alone. It seemed that the national anthem had become "Brother, Can You Spare a Dime?" Shantytowns made of cardboard and corrugated metal popped up on urban fringes. They were nicknamed Hoovervilles, for President Herbert Hoover, who was blamed for the crisis.

Even nature seemed to conspire against Americans. In good years when it rained in the Oklahoma-Texas Panhandle, country farmers plowed the grasslands under. The bad years came in the 1930s, and the winds tore at land left exposed by dying crops. The loose soil blew into big "black blizzards" or "rollers." The region became known as the Dust Bowl.

The Dust Bowl's soil was swept airborne—some of it settling on ships 300 miles out in the Atlantic Ocean. Soil in the Southeast was heading for the ocean, too. It was washed out by rains running across abused farmland. Fertile soil came off in sheets, especially on hillsides of naked, plowed ground. Hard rains cut a nick in the soil, then a notch, then a slash, then a gully. Gullies linked to gullies, and miniature Grand Canyons webbed nightmarish landscapes across the South.

Erosion resulted from too little water in some parts of the country, too much in others. What happened was no mystery. By 1935 Congress had passed the Soil Conservation Act. In 1939 Hugh Hammond Bennett wrote in Soil Conservation: "National habits of waste in this country have nowhere been exhibited more flagrantly than in the use of agricultural land."

A large influx of farmers were forced off their farms and into the Pacific region. Demand for lumber, the most popular wood produce from the nation's forests, plunged when the Depression halted housing construction. Immigration from abroad declined dramatically as Europeans thought twice about hitching their wagons to the American star.

OPPOSITE: *A common sight during the Depression: A long line of people wait in a breadline not far from the Brooklyn Bridge in New York City.*

The NEW DEAL

Picking Up the Pieces

Americans were hard hit by the Depression. Rightly or wrongly, they largely blamed President Herbert Hoover and replaced him with Franklin Delano Roosevelt, who ran on the promise that if he were elected, the federal government would end the Depression. "I pledge myself," he said, "to a new deal for the American people." He declared in his inaugural address on March 4, 1933: "The only thing we have to fear is fear itself."

FDR's frenetic first hundred days introduced new policies at a breakneck pace. These initiatives were revolutionary. He completed the rescue of the banking system with deposit insurance, regulated the stock exchanges, coordinated the faltering rail system, and went off the gold standard to raise prices. He sent $500 million to the states for direct relief, saved a fifth of all home owners from foreclosure, and refinanced farm mortgages. Perhaps the most far-reaching programs of the New Deal were the Social Security measures of 1935 and 1939, which provided old-age and widows' benefits, unemployment compensation, and disability insurance.

The government established the Tennessee Valley Authority (TVA) to tap the rivers of a seven-state area and supply cheap electricity, prevent floods, improve navigation, and introduce new farming methods. The last act, the National Industrial Recovery Act (NIRA), fostered partnership between business and the state.

FDR's New Deal included an alphabet soup of employment programs designed to put Americans back to work. The Public Works Administration,

or PWA, set up under the National Industrial Recovery Act, hired workers to build projects ranging from New York's Lincoln Tunnel to the University of New Mexico's library. New schools, courthouses, and hospitals sprang up everywhere. Not everyone felt that such reform projects were the answer. Critics complained that the federal government had too much control over business and spent too much money.

Nevertheless the PWA and other programs continued to generate millions of jobs. In 1935 the Works Progress Administration (WPA), under Harry Hopkins, aimed to employ many in building golf courses, playgrounds, parks, and airports for communities across the country. Congress appropriated a healthy $4,880,000,000 to provide work for the country's vast army of unemployed men. The money had a "pump-priming" effect on the economy and the private sector.

Hopkins also developed programs for authors, artists, and musicians. Writers hired by the Federal Writers' Project (FWP) researched and wrote guidebooks to the states and regions. They also were put to work indexing newspapers, researching sociological and historical questions, and organizing historical archives. Unemployed artists went to work for the Federal Arts Project (FAP) in hundreds of public buildings, including schools and post offices, painting murals and sculpting statues. Musicians launched community symphony orchestras and singing groups.

The Civilian Conservation Corps (CCC) put to work 2.5 million unemployed youths by the end

of the decade; they built roads and bridges in national parks, planted trees, and constructed dams all over the country. One historian noted that "the CCC left its monuments in the preservation and purification of the land, the water, the forests, and the young men of America." The typical CCC enrollee was between 18 and 19 years old, had completed eight years of schooling, and had been without a job for seven months. "We Can Take It" was the unofficial motto of the young men of the CCC. The program was disbanded on June 30, 1942, seven months after the U.S. entry into World War II.

By June 1943, when it was terminated officially, the WPA had spent $11 billion on nearly 1.5 million projects, giving work to more than 8,500,000 unemployed Americans. In eight years those Americans had built, repaired, or improved 853 airports, 8,192 parks, and 125,110 public buildings; they had also laid out 651,087 miles of highways, roads, and streets.

THE FOUR FREEDOMS

In the future days . . . we look forward to a world founded upon four essential human freedoms. The first is freedom of speech and expression— everywhere in the world. The second is freedom of every person to worship God in his own way—everywhere in the world.

The third is freedom from want, which, translated into world terms, means economic understandings which will secure to every nation a healthy peacetime life for its inhabitants—everywhere in the world.

The fourth is freedom from fear, which, translated into world terms, means a world-wide reduction of armaments to such a point and in such a thorough fashion that no nation will be in a position to commit an act of physical aggression against any neighbor—anywhere in the world.

–President Franklin Delano Roosevelt, 1941

OPPOSITE: *Part of the "American Guide Series," this pamphlet on skiing was one of the many writing pieces sponsored by the Federal Writers' Project.*

ABOVE: *Under the hot summer sun, members of the Civilian Conservation Corps (CCC) work the fields of a farm in Prince George's County, Maryland, in 1935.*

On the RESERVATION

The Bureau of Indian Affairs

With guns and horses, tribes of Native Americans were usually viewed as a threat to white settlers in the West during the 19th century. Gold mines, oil fields, and an abundance of rich farmland drew settlers onto earth that was formerly inhabited by Indians. Railroads spanned the prairies; from train windows, travelers shot the buffalo upon which Plains people relied, leaving the carcasses to rot. Armies corralled tribes onto reservations.

By the Civil War's end in 1865, nearly 20,000 soldiers manning western forts stood ready to subdue the natives. As the Army struggled to contain Apache and Navajo in New Mexico, determined Sioux under Red Cloud closed the Bozeman Trail, dictating peace terms to U.S. troops at Fort Laramie in 1868.

Mere paper would not avert a nation's will. Soon armed columns began carving inroads into Indian refuges. Each side tasted calamity: Lt. Col.

George Custer's "last stand" in 1876 at Little Big Horn took all the lives of his men. Chief Joseph and 250 Nez Perce warriors in 1877 refused to submit to U.S. authority; they held off 5,000 U.S. troops for a 1,700-mile flight. The Sioux made one final stand at the Battle of Wounded Knee in 1890 in South Dakota. More than 200 men, women, and children were killed by U.S. forces. When the dust settled and the bodies were removed, U.S. dominion sprawled unchallenged across the breadth of North America.

Reformers and missionaries sought to wean Indians from tribal customs and to assimilate them into mainstream society. Under the Dawes Act of 1887, termed the Indian Magna Carta by humanitarians, reservations were parceled out to individuals, and the "surplus" lands were sold off. The Indian Reorganization Act reversed Dawes in 1934 and signaled the kindling of a new desire— to preserve America's native culture. But by then two-thirds of America's remaining Indian property had passed into white hands.

Since its creation in 1824, the Bureau of Indian Affairs (BIA)—once an instrument of federal policies to subjugate and assimilate the tribes and their people—has tried to manage America's Native Americans amid shifting philosophies. Conferral of citizenship on Indians after World War I improved access to legal redress, but the unique status of tribes cast questions of title in a jurisprudential twilight zone.

In the thirties, FDR's "Indian New Deal" under BIA head John Collier introduced congressional measures to protect reservations and to forestall the erosion of aboriginal customs. The Indian Reorganization Act halted allotment of tribal lands to individuals and encouraged native religious practices, including the controversial consumption of peyote in the Southwest. Increased public interest sparked a renaissance in such neglected arts as weaving, pottery making, sculpture, and crafting jewelry and masks.

Still, Collier maintained policies of assimilating Indians into American culture. Though devised with good intentions, these infuriated Indians. Assimilation became synonymous with the death of their culture. "How can we plan our future when the Indian Bureau threatens to wipe us out as a race?" asked a tribal chairman.

During the 1950s Collier's successors tried to reverse his programs, urging an end to reservations, to federal acknowledgment of tribes, and to special treatment of Native Americans. Federal relocation brought thousands of Native Americans into the cities, where it was thought enhanced job prospects would improve their welfare. These policies, it was thought, would "free" Indians by speeding their absorption into mainstream society. In practice it helped free land for further exploitation.

Policy changed again in the 1960s. Some ignored tribes were officially recognized, and many land claims were settled. Yet in the areas of wealth, education, and longevity, descendants of the earliest Americans still lagged behind all other major ethnic groups, falling well below national averages. Alcoholism and unemployment plagued many on and off the reservations.

Native American groups staged demonstrations and armed takeovers to focus attention on their people's unrest. In 1968 the American Indian Movement was founded, and in 1969 members seized Alcatraz Island, a former penitentiary in San Francisco Bay, for 19 months. They declared the site to be "more than suitable for an Indian Reservation. . . . It would be fitting and symbolic that ships from all over the world, entering the Golden Gate, would first see Indian land, and thus be reminded of the true history of this nation." In 1973, 200 group members occupied the Wounded Knee battle site to protest treatment of Native Americans. The Indians laid down their arms after shots were exchanged with federal marshals.

OPPOSITE: *In 1923, the Pueblo Indians sent this delegation, posed before the U.S. Capitol, to Washington, D.C., to testify before the Senate Lands Committee.*
NEXT: *In the early 1900s, a group of historic reenactors depicted the Battle of Wounded Knee in South Dakota. Here a Native encampment can be seen as a group of U.S. soldiers lines up in the distance.*

WORLD WAR TWO

The Greatest Conflict

A world again at war had left few nations neutral in 1941 when Japan attacked Pearl Harbor and drew the U.S. into the conflict. The alliances that bound the warring nations had been taking shape for decades." We are alive, rudely awakened," wrote a young newspaper editor, Jonathan Daniels. Pearl Harbor acted on the Depression-ridden nation "like a reverse earthquake," wrote *Time* magazine, "that in one terrible jerk shook everything disjointed, distorted, askew back into place." The United States declared war on Japan, and Germany declared war on the United States, drawing the nation into the Second World War.

When Japan seized Manchuria from rebellion-torn China in 1931, some leaders spoke out, but none chose to act. While Hitler armed his new Germany, the allies who had beaten the old Germany watched, nervous but disunited. Many wanted to appease the aggressors, allowing them a few conquests in hopes they would not seek more.

But they did. Japan sought to rule "Greater East Asia." Italy claimed Ethiopia in 1935 and Albania in 1939. Germany and Italy, linked to form the Axis powers, grew bolder. Germany seized Austria, Czechoslovakia, Poland, Denmark, Norway, the Netherlands, Belgium— and, in 1940, France. The Nazis ruled half of France; their French collaborators at Vichy, the other half.

As Europe exploded into war, Japan joined the Axis alliance and seized more European-held lands in Asia and the Pacific Ocean. The world took sides. From Denmark's 15,000 troops to America's 12 million, the Allies mustered a mighty force to face the Axis nations in fighting that spanned the globe.

Following the shock of the attack on Pearl Harbor, the Americans found their Pacific forces crippled, with many sailors and marines killed and many ships sunk or disabled. Japan, on the other hand, held much of the Pacific Ocean. Its rule reached some 4,500 miles from its mainland in Asia to the Solomon and Gilbert Islands. The American Navy scored an early victory at the Battle of Midway in 1942 as carrier-based planes defeated a Japanese fleet sent to seize the island as a base, effectively halting the Japanese Pacific offensive and serving as a turning point in the War.

The Japanese lost four of five heavy carriers in the battle. During a six-month stretch of 1942–43, the Guadalcanal campaign built on the advantage created by Midway; the campaign forced the Japanese to begin a retreat from which they never recovered. Losses were heavy on both sides, but the U.S. was able to replace ships and airplanes; the Japanese were not. Before long, Americans were fighting from island to island, or "leapfrogging"—one thrust headed toward the Philippines, another through the central Pacific to bring troops and bombers within range of Tokyo.

American troops had to bide their time before joining the fighting in Europe. Months of preparation were needed before they could invade Hitler's stronghold. Finally, on June 6, 1944, U.S. and British troops crossed the English Channel and struggled ashore on Normandy's beaches. They came in nearly 5,000 ships and landing craft; 11,000 planes provided cover over-

head; troop strength numbered some 176,000. Their invasion covered nearly 60 miles of coastline and met fierce resistance from the Germans. After a few days of fighting, the Allies secured a foothold, and within seven weeks more than a million men had landed. Throughout the rest of 1944 the Americans advanced, liberating Paris and then sweeping the Germans out of France.

By September Belgium and Luxembourg had been liberated. In mid-December a strong German counterattack—the Battle of the Bulge—pushed the Americans back briefly, but in the spring of 1945 the offensive went forward again. On April 25, American soldiers advancing to the east and Russian soldiers fighting their way west met near the German town of Torgau. Five days later, with Russians fighting Germans in the streets of Berlin, Hitler committed suicide in his bunker. A week later the war in Europe was over.

In the Pacific, by the summer of 1944 the Americans had advanced close enough to reach Japan by air. Japanese cities began to feel the fury

of American bombs. Over the following months, Japan's situation became hopeless, but the country's military leaders wanted to fight to the end to resist an invasion of their homeland.

Islands like Iwo Jima and Okinawa saw bloody battles as the Allies drove by land, sea, and air toward Japan. On February 19, 1945, after 72 days of continuous, if somewhat ineffectual, air strikes, 60,000 U.S. Marines went ashore on Iwo Jima. The operation used in total 800 warships, and sent 110,000 men ashore, supported by another 220,000 men on the water. The

OPPOSITE: *Created by Norman Rockwell in 1943, this cover of the* Saturday Evening Post *depicts a woman in "Rosie the Riveter" coveralls. Women became an important part of the industrial workforce during World War II.*
ABOVE: *On December 7, 1941, Japanese planes carried out a devastating attack on the United States forces stationed at Pearl Harbor, Hawaii. Here, sailors watch as U.S.S.* Shaw *explodes in the center background.*

island's capture was to have taken 14 days. In the end, it took 36 days, and made casualties of a third of the Marine force: 5,931 dead, 17,372 wounded. The words of Fleet commander Adm. Chester W. Nimitz are inscribed on the monument to the battle outside Washington, D.C.: "Uncommon Valor was a Common Virtue."

On August 6, 1945, an American bomber, the *Enola Gay,* dropped an atomic bomb on the city of Hiroshima. It blotted out the city in a blinding flash. Three days later another bomb was dropped on Nagasaki. Five days later Japan surrendered, and World War Two was over.

On the domestic front, patriotism meant going to work as much as going to battle. More than eight million more civilians were employed in 1944 than in 1939, and 11 million others were in uniform. The ranks of the unemployed—9.5 million had been out of work in 1939—were absorbed. By 1942 U.S. industrial output equaled the combined production of the Axis powers. By 1944 it doubled it.

The workweek increased from 38 to 45 hours, and industrial output grew—by 132 percent. New plants, new production techniques, and information pooling increased efficiency, and productivity grew—by 11 percent. The government went into debt (through war bonds) to keep the economy armed, fueled, and running. The government made more personal income subject to taxation and introduced a withholding tax. Although the tax base was broader than ever, taxes paid less than half the cost of the war.

More than three million American women worked in war production, and by 1945 some 258,000 served in the armed forces. The culture of the postwar era expected that real-life Rosie the Riveters would leave the factories now that peace prevailed. For many women the independence, the pay, and the respect were not soon forgotten.

American children helped the war effort, too. They grew vegetables for the family in "victory gardens." They collected scrap paper, tin cans, foil from chewing-gum wrappers, and other materials to be used in making planes, tanks, and weapons. They loaned part of their allowance to the government to help pay for the war. Each week millions of schoolchildren bought a 25-cent stamp to paste in a special book. When the book was filled, it would be traded for a $25 Defense Savings Bond.

Old tires, doormats, and raincoats went to the war effort when President Franklin D. Roosevelt asked the nation to contribute rubber, critically short after Japanese conquests in the Far East. The response totaled 450,000 tons. Gas rationing followed, its intent less to save gas than to reduce tire wear. Growing domestic production of synthetic rubber ended the crisis.

With Liberty ships, mass production of freighters to supply troops across four oceans became a reality. Construction time was finally cut to 111 hours. More than 2,700 Liberty ships were built at about 1.6 million dollars each; 195 were lost at sea.

As for bombers, load-carrying capacity required ever larger sizes, stronger airframes, and more powerful engines. Bomber development pointed the way toward civilian airliners. The first American-designed bomber, the Martin MB-1, served from 1918 to 1923. The B-17 Flying Fortress, the first all-metal, four-engine U.S. bomber, was later derived from an airliner design; 12,000 of the craft flew in World War II.

Mobilization was not without its confusions, dislocations, profiteering, and plain miscalculations. Due to wartime paranoia, in March 1942, the U.S. War Relocation Authority oversaw the forced evacuation of Japanese Americans from their homes to 10 internment camps located in the western United States. Nearly 120,000 Japanese Americans spent much of the war in these camps.

Early in the war, the rush to mobilize was so overpowering that too much in the way of scarce materials was being used to build factories; not enough was being reserved to build munitions. U.S. industrialists understood the geopolitics. Their factories were keeping Allied armies supplied in western Europe, in the Soviet Union, and in China—as well as fully provisioning a U.S. military force of more than 16 million. It was a performance to make even Soviet leader Joseph

Stalin raise a glass to toast American production, without which the Allies "never could have won the war."

Toward the war's end, another concern arose: Would victory lead to depression? Between May and August 1945, jobs in the aircraft, ammunition, and shipbuilding industries dropped by nearly 50 percent, or 1.2 million people. Two and a half million more war workers were laid off in September 1945. A million and a half military personnel were demobilized by the year's end. Yet the economy did not collapse. Swift reconversion to peacetime industry only began to meet a huge backlog of demand. Postwar production instead turned out cars, appliances, houses, and babies.

BELOW: *Two prisoners at a German concentration camp support a listing comrade during roll call. Fainting was often used as an excuse by the Germans to execute inmates during World War Two.*

PEARL HARBOR ATTACKED

Yesterday, December 7, 1941—a date which will live in infamy—the United States of America was suddenly and deliberately attacked by naval and air forces of the empire of Japan.... The attack yesterday on the Hawaiian Islands has caused severe damage to American naval and military forces. I regret to tell you that very many American lives have been lost . . . .

As Commander in Chief of the Army and Navy I have directed that all measures be taken in our defense. Always will our whole nation remember the character of the onslaught against us. No matter how long it may take us to over come this premeditated invasion, the American people, in their righteous might, will win through to absolute victory . . . .

Hostilities exist. There is no blinking at the fact that our people, our territory, and our interests are in grave danger. With confidence in our armed forces, with the unbounding determination of our people, we will gain the inevitable triumph. So help us God.

—President Franklin Delano Roosevelt

The MANHATTAN PROJECT

Igniting the Air

We knew the world would not be the same. A few people laughed, a few people cried. Most people were silent. I remembered the line from the Hindu scripture, the Bhagavad gita . . . 'I am become Death, the destroyer of worlds.' I suppose we all thought that, one way or another." Robert Oppenheimer was reflecting on the vision he saw as he looked upon the havoc he helped to release at a desolate spot in the New Mexico desert in July 1945. The Manhattan Project unlocked the mysteries of the atom, but it also introduced to the world the most destructive weapon known to man.

It was born in the midst of World War II. Much of the early research for the project was done in New York City by the Manhattan Engineer District of the U.S. Army Corps of Engineers, giving it the name the Manhattan Project. It would take four years of work, from 1942 to 1945, and $1.8 billion in 1940s dollars to design and create an atomic bomb. The Project was unusual in that it involved cooperation among scientists, military officers, and civilians. Conducted in great secrecy, it efficiently produced the desired result.

Test director Kenneth T. Bainbridge settled on an isolated site near Alamogordo, New Mexico, a valley called the Jornada del Muerto, to build the bomb. Oppenheimer selected the name by which the site would be known: Trinity. On July 16, 1945, the first test was conducted. Observers about 10,000 yards from the blast site, wearing welders' glasses and suntan lotion, watched the equivalent of 20,000 tons of TNT explode. At ground zero the temperature rose to between 3,000 and 4,000 degrees Celsius.

While the successful test occurred at Alamogordo, the rest of the world was oblivious to developments there. President Roosevelt suddenly died and his successor, President Harry Truman, who had never heard of the bomb, had to be brought into the undertaking and fully briefed. After the German surrender in Europe, the world's attention turned to the Pacific front.

Disagreements arose about whether the bomb was truly necessary to end the war. And if it was, should it be used on only military targets—or on a Japanese city? Some argued that the Japanese should be shown a demonstration of the bomb's power; perhaps they would be cowed into surrender. Others insisted that only the destruction of the Japanese homeland would provide the shock that would lead to their surrender.

In the end, the proponents of the bomb won out: Its use, they believed, would save thousands of Allied lives by removing the necessity of invading the Japanese islands. President Truman approved the bombs' use. On August 6, 1945, a B-29 named the *Enola Gay*—for the pilot's mother—dropped the bomb "Little Boy" on the city of Hiroshima. It missed its primary target by several hundred feet but still destroyed much of the city and killed 80,000 people; many thousands more would later die from radiation poisoning. Three days later the bomb "Fat Man" was dropped on Nagasaki, killing 60,000 people. Japan surrendered. A new age had begun.

OPPOSITE: *On August 9, 1945, a mushroom cloud rose over Nagasaki, the second Japanese city struck by an atomic bomb, which took 60,000 lives.*

1 9 5 0
THROUGH
PRESENT

DECADES *of* CHANGE

A MERICA IS A LARGE FRIENDLY DOG IN a small room," Arnold Toynbee wrote in 1954. "Every time it wags its tail it knocks over a chair."

During the second half of the 20th century America seemed to be constantly knocking over chairs. American armies went to Korea and Vietnam and Iraq. The Peace Corps went everywhere. American streets became zones of unrest, as citizens protested wars and inequalities. Assassins' bullets felled revered leaders. At the same time, steps were taken into space, the final frontier. New technologies led to medical breakthroughs and, on the Internet, revolutions in the dissemination of knowledge.

When 1976 rolled around, it was time to observe the Bicentennial of the longstanding democratic nation. The president of France came to help celebrate what Lafayette had helped start. Valéry Giscard d'Estaing said: "It is not for us to predict what role you will actually play in the future. That . . . remains to be heard. I assure you of this: We are all listening."

Americans huddled nervously around their radios and TVs when the new millennium arrived, fearing the worst and hoping, as always, for the best. The new century brought some of both.

In 1900 Scottish critic William Archer had written, "The United States is a self-conscious, clearly defined, and heroically vindicated idea, in whose further vindication the whole world is concerned. . . . The United States of America, let us say, is a rehearsal for the United States of Europe, nay, of the world."

NASA photography reveals the bright city lights that illuminate the U.S. by night.

SMALL SCREENS

The Birth of Television

Watching the first *See It Now* TV episode on November 18, 1951, viewers saw Edward R. Murrow pointing to two television monitors, one showing the Atlantic Ocean, the other the Pacific. Each coast could see the other one—the continent of North America shrunk to fit a small screen.

TV's largest early studio was opened in 1946 by DuMont, which linked New York and Washington, D.C., in the first commercial network. DuMont soon lost out to NBC, CBS, and ABC. Transcontinental TV broadcasting began in 1951. AT&T's new coast-to-coast TV link (shared by the networks) transmitted President Harry Truman's address to the San Francisco peace conference that officially ended the war with Japan.

Television changed American society in many ways. In 1954 frozen TV dinners hit the market, and families found themselves perched in the flickering darkness, eating and watching TV at the same time.

Many consider the 1950s the Golden Age of American television. Vaudeville, in essence, made the leap from the stage to the small screen as variety shows featured comic skits, acrobats, and singing and dancing. Milton Berle—Uncle Miltie—first came on the air in June 1948, and reigned supreme throughout the fifties, often in drag. *Your Show of Shows* with Sid Caesar debuted in February 1950 and ran until June 1954. Ninety minutes long, it featured Imogene Coca, Carl Reiner, and Howard Morris. Writers for the show included such young talents as Woody

Allen, Mel Brooks, Neil Simon, and Larry Gelbart. The smooth and relaxed Perry Como hosted an hour-long show between 1955 and 1963. "Dream Along With Me," he would sing at the beginning of each show. The Peter Gennaro dancers and the Ray Charles singers were regulars. The *Colgate Comedy Hour* was first to be telecast in color, on November 22, 1953. It featured rotating hosts such as Martin and Lewis and Abbott and Costello. *Your Hit Parade*, from 1950 until 1959, presented the seven most popular songs of the week. On September 9, 1956, pop singer and early American idol Elvis Presley appeared on the Ed Sullivan variety show, which showed the famous hip-swiveler only from the waist up.

Today premiered on January 14, 1952, and *Tonight*, with Steve Allen, in 1954. Several studios presented 90-minute original dramas each week. Paddy Chayefsky's *Marty* was broadcast in May 1953, with Rod Steiger as the lonely Bronx butcher. Later in the fifties westerns became popular. *Gunsmoke*, the first adult western, ran from 1955 to 1975 on CBS. *Bonanza* had Sunday nights on NBC, in color on the Ponderosa, from 1959 until 1973.

In an emerging quiz show scandal, Columbia University Professor Charles Van Doren admitted to a U.S. House Subcommittee that he had been coached for appearances on NBC's *Twenty-One* in 1956, on which he had won $129,000. His name became synonymous with "cheater," and the networks scrambled to clean up all their quiz shows.

Ownership of television sets had become widespread by the early 1960s. Most local stations depended on affiliation with one of the three major networks. The medium's novelty was color, and in December 1966 consumers for the first time bought more color than black-and-white sets.

In the 1960s, TV became a powerful player in politics and current events. Politicians quickly learned the benefits of appearing on television, though some learned more slowly than others. In September 1960 candidates Richard Nixon and John Kennedy held the first presidential debate on TV, an occasion considered disastrous for the unphotogenic Nixon, whose five o'clock shadow famously cost him votes.

In 1963 President Kennedy's assassin was also assassinated—on live TV. Four days of nonstop coverage that started with three shots in Dallas became for many, including writer Marya Mannes, "total involvement . . . I stayed before the set, knowing—as millions knew—that I must give myself over entirely to an appalling tragedy, and that to evade it was a treason of the spirit."

Another generation watched the Vietnam "living-room war" in all its nightly news horror. And on July 20, 1969, the world watched man's first steps on the moon—a giant leap for television and its audience.

BELOW: *Desi Arnaz gives his real-life wife, Lucille Ball, a peck on the cheek on the set of their television show,* I Love Lucy.

OPPOSITE: *Quiz shows had great popularity. A guest and his expert confer inside an isolation booth during a session of* The $64,000 Question, *around 1957. The quiz-show genre disappeared for a number of years when some shows were found to be rigged.*

STEMMING *the* COMMUNIST TIDE

The Korean Conflict

After World War II, the U.S. and the Soviet Union agreed to joint occupation of Korea. Two young American colonels—one of them Dean Rusk—had half an hour to find a place to cut Korea in half. They chose the 38th Parallel, which put Korea's capital Seoul and 21 million people in the South and 9 million people and most of its industry in the North.

Edgy about communism, the Americans chose 70-year-old Syngman Rhee, who had been living in the U.S. since 1904, to govern the South; a Moscow-trained communist, 33-year-old Kim Il Sung, was put in place in the North. The U.S. and the Soviet Union withdrew from Korea in 1948, leaving Rhee and Sung in power. It was a situation bound to fail. When Stalin gave Kim

Il Sung permission to "liberate" the South, North Korean troops poured across the 38th Parallel.

"By God," said President Truman, on June 24, 1950, "I'm going to let them have it." On June 27 the United Nations Security Council voted 7 to 1 to join the war on South Korea's side. It was the first time the UN had attempted to uphold international law by force of arms. The U.S. would contribute the bulk of the forces, followed by South Korea, Britain, Canada, Turkey, and Australia. American troops departed for the Korean Peninsula.

The fighting lasted from June 25, 1950, to July 27, 1953. In the beginning, the North Korean troops nearly swept the defending armies of South Koreans and American soldiers off the peninsula, capturing the capital of Seoul on June 27. To lead American troops, Truman sent 70-year-old Gen. Douglas MacArthur, who mobilized American ground forces from Japan. But they were underequipped, both militarily and emotionally, for the fight. They finally dug in, with their backs to the sea, at the southeastern port of Pusan. The tide was turned by a masterstroke by MacArthur, who made an amphibious landing at Seoul's seaport of Inchon, 200 miles behind the backs of the North Koreans. The 1st Marine Division retook Seoul.

The next phase of fighting took MacArthur and his men across the 38th Parallel into North Korea. But when they approached North Korea's border with China, thousands of Chinese troops, who had been waiting in North Korea's canyons and desolate valleys, attacked on all sides, often at night. They destroyed South Korean regiments and forced the Americans to retreat south across the Chongchon River.

Farther east, another American force was beaten back in the longest retreat in American history, some 120 miles. Unflappable General Oliver Smith, asked about the retreat, said, "Gentlemen, we're not retreating. We are just advancing in a different direction." American counterattacks pushed the Chinese back above the 38th Parallel and there a long, futile war of attrition began.

Peace talks began on July 10, 1951, but fighting continued for two more years. America lost 54,246 troops, the Chinese perhaps a million, South Korea 47,000. At the end there were still two Koreas, separated by the 38th Parallel.

A sidebar to the Korean drama played out between President Truman and his commander, Douglas MacArthur. MacArthur, approaching the end of a half-century career, chafed under civilian control. He argued vociferously for total war on Communist China. He requested 26 atomic bombs to be dropped on North Korea and China. He repeatedly disobeyed orders: bombing bridges over the Yalu River when directed to not bomb within five miles of the border; giving press interviews that undermined administration policy; publicly disagreeing with UN policies regarding reunification of the Koreas. He was frighteningly ready to risk global nuclear war.

Finally Truman had enough and relieved MacArthur of his command. Truman wrote, "I deeply regret that it becomes my duty as Commander-in-Chief of the United States military forces to replace you as Supreme Commander, Allied Powers." MacCarthur left Korea and returned to the U.S. in April 1951.

When MacArthur arrived in San Francisco, half a million people lined the streets to cheer him, and in New York seven million attended a ticker tape parade. He gave an emotional 34-minute address to Congress. Truman described it as "nothing but a bunch of damn bullshit." At the end, MacArthur said: "I still remember the refrain of one of the most popular barrack ballads of that day, which proclaimed, most proudly, that 'Old soldiers never die. They just fade away.' And like the soldier of the ballad, I now close my military career and just fade away—an old soldier who tried to do his duty as God gave him the light to see that duty. . . . Goodbye."

OPPOSITE: *Gen. of the Army Douglas MacArthur, Maj. Gen. Courtney Whitney, Lt. Gen. Matthew B. Ridgway, and Maj. Gen. William B. Kean (right to left) assemble at the front lines near Suwon, Korea, in January 1951.*

FIGHT *for* CIVIL RIGHTS

The Early Stirrings

The first years following the Civil War brought little economic change to landless freedmen trapped in the sharecropping system, though new political power gave hope to many. During Reconstruction, blacks organized to win elective office in the South, but their victories were short-lived. By 1876, with the "redemption" of the South by traditional Democrats and the end of Reconstruction by northern Republicans, the fight for racial equality fell by the wayside.

In the late 1870s, many southern states passed legislation that legalized racial segregation. This system of laws became popularly known as "Jim Crow" laws, named for a minstral routine popular in the 19th century. The Supreme Court codified these laws in *Plessy v. Ferguson* (1896), the case that popularized the practice of "separate but equal." The circumstances that followed for black Americans was hardly equal or fair.

By 1908 all southern states had effectively barred blacks from the polls through such devices as literacy tests, property qualifications, and poll taxes. Separation of the races by law was still the rule in 1950. In many states blacks remained cut off from whites in virtually every phase of existence. The Supreme Court's "separate but equal" doctrine applied to public transportation and accommodations, yet it was used as a rationale to establish broad unequal segregation. Local ordinances, usually more restrictive than state laws, sanctioned what had already been the practice.

Newspaper reports of alleged black crimes contributed to vigilantism by whites. Charges involving rape or murder by black men were frequently sensationalized. Lurid accounts of such attacks were used to justify lynchings, especially in the South. Of the 4,743 lynchings reported between 1882 and 1958, nearly 75 percent of the victims were black.

In the early 20th century groups like the National Association for the Advancement of Colored People (NAACP) pursued civil rights, defending victims of race riots and protesting discrimination against black soldiers during World War One. From its founding in 1909, the NAACP used nonviolent political and legal actions and prompted many important civil rights acts and Supreme Court decisions. For example, in 1944, it was declared in *Smith v. Allwright* that primary

---

BROWN V. BOARD OF EDUCATION

In approaching this problem, we cannot turn the clock back to 1868 when the [Fourteenth] Amendment was adopted. We must consider public education in the light of its full development and its present place in American life throughout the Nation. Only in this way can it be determined if segregation in public schools deprives these plaintiffs of the equal protection of the laws . . .

Whatever may have been the extent of psychological knowledge at the time of Plessy v. Ferguson, this finding [that segregation has a tendency to retard the educational and mental development of black children] is amply supported by modern authority. Any language in Plessy v. Ferguson contrary to this finding is rejected.

We conclude that in the field of public education the doctrine of "separate but equal" has no place. Separate educational facilities are inherently unequal. ■

elections could not be closed to blacks. In 1948 restrictive covenants requiring homeowners to sell only to whites could not be enforced in the courts, decided in *Shelley v. Kraemer*. In 1954 public school segregation was ruled unconstitutional in *Brown v. Board of Education, Topeka, Kansas.* This landmark decision demolished *Plessy v. Ferguson* and established a new precedent. Educational desegregation was not a smooth process. In 1957, President Dwight D. Eisenhower ordered federal troops to Little Rock, Arkansas, to enforce an integration order for nine black students in Central High School.

To gain these crucial legal advances and changes, civil rights activists worked through many channels. Groups like the NAACP fought by legal means while other activists used public protests as their means to change. From the 1940s through the early 1970s, blacks first used civil disobedience to assert their rights. Peaceably enough, in 1955 and 1956, blacks boycotted the Montgomery, Alabama, bus system after Rosa Parks was arrested for refusing to surrender her seat to a white man. In 1961 the Congress of Racial Equality (CORE) dispatched freedom riders throughout the South to test whether the transportation facilities there were in fact desegregated. And in 1963 more than 250,000 blacks and whites participated in a peaceful march on Washington, D.C., for civil rights.

By the mid-1960s there were often outbreaks of violence by those frustrated by the delay in being granted full civil rights. A race-related riot raged for six days in the Watts area of Los Angeles in June 1965. Two years later reports of police brutality in Newark, N.J., sparked riots that claimed the lives of 21 blacks and marked the beginning of the "long hot summer." In Michigan,

---

ABOVE: *Eerily matter-of-fact, a crowd gathers on a hot August evening in Marion, Indiana, in 1930 to gawk at a lynching. Between 1889 and 1918, some 2,500 blacks were lynched in the U.S., 50 of them women.*

COLORED
WAITING ROOM

PRIVATE PROPERTY
NO PARKING
iving through or Turning Around

A COACH COMP

Detroit's black neighborhoods were decimated during a week-long interracial clash in July.

Some activists advocated a nonviolent approach to civil rights. "Put on your marching shoes. Walk with me into a new dignity," Martin Luther King, Jr., had challenged his followers. He had grown up in Atlanta, a bold and persistent child. He dreamed of help for the poor—on dirt farms in the South, in ghettos in the North. After the bus protest in Montgomery, which he helped organize, he became a central figure in the civil rights movement. He preached nonviolence and conciliation. During the March on Washington, in 1963, he held a huge audience spellbound as he described his vision of America. In 1964 he won the Nobel Peace Prize.

Legislative gains in civil rights came in the late 1950s and early 1960s. In 1957 the Civil Rights Commission, a bipartisan advisory committee, was created by Congress. The Civil Rights Act of 1957, the first civil rights legislation of the 20th century, pledged that voting rights would be enforced by federal officials if courts found a "pattern or practice" of disenfranchising blacks in a state or locality. In 1962, discrimination in housing projects funded by the federal government was banned by a presidential executive order.

Legal demolition of voting barriers came with the Civil Rights Act of 1964 and the Voting Rights Act of 1965. The Voting Rights Act eliminated literacy tests, provided for federal registrars to enroll blacks unlawfully deprived of the right to vote, and specifically outlawed intimidation of blacks who were trying to register or to vote. A few years later, 1968's Federal Fair Housing Law ended racial discrimination in the sale and rental of most housing. The fight against racism would continue throughout the 20th century, but these crucial beginnings laid the foundation for the years to come.

LEFT: *At this bus station in Durham, North Carolina, in 1940, prominent signs designate separate waiting rooms for black Americans.*

TRAGEDY *and* LOSS

Assassination Plagues the Nation

On April 3, 1968, Dr. Martin Luther King, Jr., gave a speech. "Like anybody, I would like to live a long life. Longevity has its place. But I'm not concerned about that now. I just want to do God's will. And He's allowed me to go up to the mountain and I've looked over, and I've seen the promised land. I may not get there with you. But I want you to know that we, as a people, will get to the promised land. And so I'm happy tonight. I'm not worried about anything. I'm not fearing any man. Mine eyes have seen the glory of the coming of the Lord."

The next morning, Dr. King stepped out onto a balcony of the Lorraine Motel in Memphis, Tennessee, and was fatally shot by a 39-year-old career criminal named James Earl Ray. The Rev. Ralph Abernathy, a friend and colleague, was at King's side in a moment, cradling his head and patting his cheek, murmuring, "This is Ralph, this is Ralph, Martin, don't be afraid."

The assassination of the peace-loving Dr. King provoked outrage throughout the country. In over 100 cities, violent riots broke out. But in Indianapolis, where Senator Robert F. Kennedy was campaigning for the presidency, the city stayed calm. Some credit Kennedy, who had been addressing a predominantly black rally in Indianapolis when he heard of King's death; he announced it to the crowd and appealed to them to uphold Dr. King's legacy of nonviolence.

Dr. King's assassination was one of a number of killings—including the earlier murder of John F. Kennedy in 1963 and later death of Robert Kennedy—in the 1960s that shook Americans to

their souls. Many wondered if the streak of violence that had haunted the country's history—from slavery and the elimination of whole tribes of Native Americans to the gunslingers of the old West—was still haunting the country. Could the American dream be unraveling?

President John F. Kennedy's death came while he was campaigning on November 23, 1963, for reelection. He and his wife, Jaqueline, rode in an open limosine as part of a motorcade in Dallas, Texas. As their car entered Dealey Plaza at 12:30 p.m., shots rang out and struck the President. A team of physicians at Dallas's Parkland Hospital fought to save his life, but the wounds were fatal. The President's death was officially announced on national television by a distraught Walter Cronkite to an audience of stunned Americans.

The assassin was a former marine named Lee Harvey Oswald. The mystery of why he would kill a President—especially one who was so revered by the American people for his vision and spirit—deepened two days later when he himself was shot by Jack Ruby, a Dallas businessman.

For four days, Americans huddled around their television sets and watched as the unbelievable drama unfolded: the assassin himself assassinated; the gathering of world leaders marching in the streets of Washington at the slain President's funeral; Kennedy's son John John saluting his father's casket. For decades following the killing, conspiracy theories abounded as Americans grappled with the idea that a single disturbed man could so profoundly alter history.

MALCOLM X

He grew up in Lansing, Michigan, as Malcolm Little. In and out of trouble and detention homes, Little moved in his early teens to Boston to live with a sister. While in prison for burglary, he joined the Nation of Islam; after his release, Little journeyed to Chicago to meet the sect's leader, Elijah Muhammad. He took the name Malcolm X—the X representing his long-lost African name.

Malcolm X began speaking on race and religion. With bitter eloquence he railed against the exploitation of blacks. He was contemptuous of the civil rights movement and rejected integration. Instead, he called for black separatism, pride, and self-reliance. Malcolm X ultimately broke with Elijah in 1963 after a pilgrimage to Mecca. There, X became convinced that Islam embraced all colors. "He was trapped somewhere between his utopian black nationalism . . . and the competing chimera of Martin Luther King's completely integrated, beloved community, and the conflict would tear him apart before it made him a saint," one historian wrote. Malcolm X was assassinated by rivals on February 21, 1965, while preparing to speak in New York. ■

Tragedy would again visit the Kennedy family in 1968, two months after the assassination of Dr. King. Robert F. Kennedy, the former attorney general, was running for the Democratic nomination for president. He campaigned hard, and by the time of the California primary, had won five out of six state primaries. But late on the day of the primary, June 5, he delivered a rousing speech to some 1,800 supporters in the ballroom of Los Angeles's Ambassador Hotel. After the speech, as he was leaving through the hotel's kitchen just after midnight, a Palestinian immigrant named Sirhan Sirhan fired eight shots and fatally struck him before horrified onlookers. Kennedy's death was another tragic loss for the nation.

OPPOSITE: *In 1964, civil rights activist Malcolm X traveled to Mecca and embraced a broader view of Islam that changed his views on race relations.*
ABOVE: *Commuting Americans read blaring headlines that document the tragic assassination of President John F. Kennedy in November 1963.*

The WAR in SOUTHEAST ASIA

Vietnam Conflict

"It was the longest war in America's history," journalist Harold Evans wrote, "in the end the most unpopular war, and the first modern war America lost . . . It destroyed the illusion of American omnipotence . . . It polarized the country as nothing had since the Civil War . . . In addition, it shattered people's faith in the honesty and credibility of government, as every administration involved systematically deceived the people."

America's involvement in the Vietnam War lasted from 1959 to 1975. The central conflict arose when the Democratic Republic of Vietnam (also called North Vietnam) wished to reunite with the Republic of Vietnam (or South Vietnam) as one communist nation. The four presidents most deeply involved with Vietnam—Eisenhower, Kennedy, Johnson, and Nixon—were haunted by a domino theory born in World War II. As Poland, France, Belgium, Holland, Norway, and Denmark had fallen to Hitler's Nazis after he was allowed to take Czechoslovakia, then surely Thailand, Burma, Malaysia, Indonesia, and perhaps even India might become communist nations if Vietnam became one. From there, communism's spread would be unstoppable. Lyndon Johnson said that if America lost Vietnam it would find itself defending the beaches of Waikiki. So American troops would go to war in far-off Southeast Asia.

It began with economic and military aid provided by the U.S. to the South Vietnamese. Secretary of State John Foster Dulles had assured the government that Americans need not die in far-off Asia—victory could be had merely by assisting the South Vietnamese. But the North Vietnamese troops—the Viet Cong—continued to infiltrate the South. President Kennedy authorized additional noncombatant military personnel, called advisers, and by the end of 1962 there were 11,000 in South Vietnam. If attacked, they were authorized to defend themselves with force.

Early in August 1964, in the Gulf of Tonkin, a U.S. destroyer reported being fired upon by North Vietnamese patrol boats. In response to the attack, President Johnson persuaded Congress to endorse the Gulf of Tonkin Resolution, authorizing the President to take "all necessary measures to repel attacks." On his orders, U.S. planes began bombing North Vietnam.

After 1965 American troops poured into the country and fighting escalated. Military leaders maintained that the war could be won with a little more material and a few more troops. It was assumed that failure by the U.S. would lessen American credibility throughout the world. By June 1965, some 50,000 American troops were

fighting with the South Vietnamese, expanding to 180,000 by year's end.

But they were having little success: U.S. military leaders were relying on outdated battle tactics. The Viet Cong used different strategies: surprise attacks, ambushes, stealth, and concealment. The U.S. sought to win with superior firepower and helicopters and increased the number of troops to 389,000 in 1967.

Then came a major surprise. At the time of the lunar new year—Tet—in 1968, the North Vietnamese and Viet Cong launched coordinated attacks throughout the South, hitting 36 major cities and towns. Even in Saigon the fighting was fierce. The casualties the North suffered were enormous but so was their victory: a growing conviction in America that the war was foolish and could not be won. Protests against it grew in volume and number. Many Americans even wondered if the U.S. was morally justified in interfering in a conflict that looked very much like a Vietnamese civil war.

While the war was raging in southeast Asia, a parallel battle was fought on the streets and campuses of the U.S. As the Vietnam war escalated, so did doubts about it at home. Into the mid-1960s, most Americans supported the involvement in Vietnam. But as the conflict continued, public opinion became bitterly divided. The U.S. had been gradually drawn into a war for reasons that were not entirely clear. Growing numbers of young people began to burn draft cards. They organized antiwar marches, wore peace symbols, waved the North Vietnamese flag.

The first antiwar protests had been tentative affairs that received little attention. One in Boston in 1965, for instance, drew only about a

---

OPPOSITE: *Protesters carry a large peace sign during a 1971 antiwar demonstration in Washington, D.C.*
ABOVE: *Two American soldiers wait for a second wave of combat helicopters to fly over during a search and destroy mission in South Vietnam.*

hundred people. The first major antiwar rally in Washington, D.C., was staged by students on April 17, 1965, just a month after the U.S. had sent its first Marines to Vietnam. About 16,000 people picketed the White House and marched on the Capitol. Only four arrests were made.

But as the war dragged on, protests grew in size and frequency. From 1967 until 1973 a major march occurred in Washington, D.C., every year, including four of the largest antiwar demonstrations in American history. On October 21, 1967, the March on the Pentagon, led by Abbie Hoffman and Jerry Rubin of the Youth International Party (or Yippies) brought about 100,000 protesters to the Pentagon, where more than 2,500 Army troops stood. The Moratorium rally on November 15, 1969, was the biggest antiwar demonstration in American history with more than 250,000 protesters—some estimates as high as 500,000—pouring down Pennsylvania Avenue and spilling onto the National Mall.

In 1969, President Richard Nixon put in place a new policy called "Vietnamization," which sounded much like the policy that had launched the war. The U.S. would provide arms, equipment, air support, and economic aid, and the South Vietnamese would fight their own battles. American field commanders were ordered to keep casualties to "an absolute minimum." In the meantime the peace talks under way between Hanoi and the U.S. in Paris made little progress.

In the spring of 1970, U.S. and South Vietnamese troops crossed the border into Cambodia to destroy Viet Cong bases there. U.S. planes over northern Laos bombed and napalmed North Vietnamese troops battling American-supported Vientiane government troops. President Nixon announced this development on April 30, 1970. Nationwide, students rallied to protest what they saw as an escalation of the war.

One of the most infamous antiwar protests came in response to Nixon's escalation. It occurred at Kent State, in Ohio. The initial demonstration so alarmed Kent's mayor that he called in the Ohio National Guard to control the student demonstrations. A thousand troops

arrived by May 3. Skirmishes broke out between the guardsman and the demonstrators, culminating in the shooting of 13 students on May 4. Four students were killed and nine wounded. Campuses all over the country exploded in rage; more than 400 shut down as two million students went on strike, furthering the political divide in the nation.

The Vietnam War protests had some influence in bringing an earlier end to the war, but the extent of that influence is still in dispute. The antiwar movement certainly benefited from unprecedented access to coverage of the war. Television brought the latest developments and atrocities into people's homes in ways that newspapers could not. The nightly bombardment of images from the war led to fatigue among the American people, who wanted an end to the conflict. By the end of 1971, U.S. withdrawal was proceeding quickly, and soon only 160,000 American troops were left.

In Paris, after years of negotiations, an agreement between the South Vietnamese communist forces, North Vietnam, South Vietnam, and the U.S. was signed on January 27, 1973. It called upon an international force to keep peace; North Vietnamese troops could remain in the South but could not be reinforced, and the South would have the right to determine its own future. All prisoners of war would be released. U.S. troops would withdraw and their bases be torn down.

In August 1973 the U.S. Congress voted against any further U.S. military activity in Indochina, and by year's end few U.S. military personnel remained there. The war took the lives of more than 58,000 U.S. soldiers and between 2 and 5 million Vietnamese. In 1975, North Vietnam invaded South Vietnam; on July 2, 1976, the two Vietnams were formally united as the Socialist Republic of Vietnam.

OPPOSITE: *Located near the Saigon River in Vietnam, a market of fruit and vegetable stands is consumed by a large fire in January 1971. Fires were much feared as many houses were highly combustible and built closely together.*

The FIRST SMALL STEPS

Space Exploration

On October 14, 1947, Air Force test pilot Chuck Yeager strapped himself into a Bell X-1 rocket—a craft shaped like a .50-caliber bullet—and dropped from under the belly of a specially modified B-29 bomber over California's Mojave Desert. When the engine ignited, the craft soon hit a speed of more than 600 miles an hour, the first time man had flown faster than the speed of sound. "It was as smooth as a baby's bottom," Yeager said. "Grandma could be up there sipping lemonade." His aplomb showed he had "the right stuff," in writer Tom Wolfe's memorable phrase—a characteristic that would survive in future astronauts as the U.S. took its first steps into outer space.

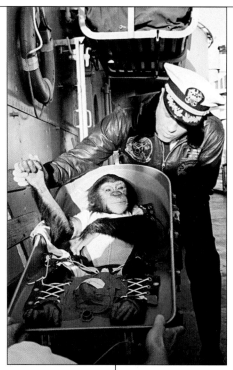

The Soviet Union launched the space age with a tiny aluminum capsule called Sputnik 1. It began orbiting the Earth and beeping its taunt back to American scientists in October 1957. The following month the Soviets took an even larger step, testing the effects of space travel on a dog, Laika, who was sent into orbit.

High schools across the nation scrambled to redo science curricula in the face of this perceived humiliation. After several explosive failures, in January 1958 the U.S. sent its own satellite into orbit, and in July created an agency to oversee the exploration of space—NASA, the National Aeronautics and Space Administration. In 1961, the U.S. sent the first hominid into space, Ham the Chimp. Still, the U.S. in the early years of exploration remained a few steps behind.

In April 1961 the Soviets scored another triumph by being first to launch a man, Yuri Gagarin, into space. The personable young cosmonaut said, "To be the first to enter the cosmos, to engage, single-handed, in an unprecedented duel with nature—could one dream of anything more?" He was the first to experience weightlessness in space, when his notebooks and pens floated loose in the Vostok capsule.

The next month Alan Shepard became the first American in space, with a 15-minute suborbital flight in a capsule named Freedom 7. Inside his nine-and-a-half-foot-tall capsule, he quickly rocketed to a speed of 5,180 mph and rose to 116.5 miles above the Earth's surface; there the engines cut off and the astronaut and his capsule hurtled through space and dropped down into the Atlantic Ocean a mere 40 miles from their target.

Within a year John Glenn circled the Earth tucked inside a Project Mercury capsule named Friendship 7. Americans stayed riveted to their television sets as a serious glitch developed during Glenn's mission. An alarm indicated that the crucial heat shield was loose and liable to come off during the fiery re-entry. To help keep the heat shield in place, Glenn was advised to keep the retro-rockets attached instead of jettisoning them. As he fell toward Earth at 15,000 mph at the end of his short mission, flaming pieces of the retropack flew past his window. But the astronaut splashed down safely nearly five hours after liftoff.

The six Mercury astronauts flew on their backs, wedged into the wide end of their bell-shaped craft. Because the quarters were cramped, all the original astronauts were less than 5 feet 11 inches tall. The next generation of American spacecraft—Gemini—were designed to transport two crewmen.

The Gemini program taught NASA skills it needed before it could land astronauts on the moon: maneuvering a spacecraft in orbit, rendezvousing with another spacecraft, and working in space outside the vehicle. Though the capsule was larger, each astronaut had less space—from 55 to 40 cubic feet—than in Mercury. Gemini accomplished a number of "firsts": the first space walk by Ed White, the first rendezvous of spacecraft, and the first manned docking with a target vehicle. During its ten missions, Gemini showed that people could live in space as long as two weeks—more than time enough to get to the Moon and back—and could accomplish tasks during space walks. For the first time, astronauts were true pilots, using onboard computers and rockets to maneuver in space.

The Apollo program built upon the success—and failures—of previous programs. It included many unmanned test missions and 12 missions with astronauts aboard: three Earth-orbiting missions (Apollo 7, 9, and Apollo-Soyuz), two lunar orbiting missions (Apollo 8 and 10), a lunar flyby

---

OPPOSITE: *Ham, the first chimpanzee to fly in space, is greeted with a handshake after his flight on the Mercury Redstone rocket in 1961.*

BELOW: *An aeronautical forebear, Chuck Yeager, broke the world's speed record in a Tell X-1A aircraft in 1953. He had been the first to break the sound barrier in 1947.*

(Apollo 13), and six moon-landing missions (Apollo 11, 12, 14, 15, 16, and 17). Two astronauts from each of the final six missions walked on the moon, the only humans yet to have set foot on another body in the solar system.

The Apollo 8 mission was launched early December 21, 1968. The three astronauts on board—Frank Borman, James Lovell, and William Anders—journeyed 200,000 miles to orbit the moon, the first humans ever to travel there. Apollo 8's mission lasted 7 days and included 10 orbits around the moon. Apollo 10, launched on May 18, 1969, was a 10-day dress rehearsal for the actual first landing. It entered orbit around the moon, and its lunar module *Snoopy* descended to within nine miles of the lunar surface with two astronauts on board. They tested the lunar module's radar and ascent engine and surveyed the landing site for Apollo 11.

Apollo 11, launched on July 16, 1969, made its historic landing on July 20, 1969. A camera in the lunar module watched and conveyed a fuzzy image back to Earth as Neil Armstrong climbed down the ladder and planted the first human footprint on the moon. "That's one small step for a man," he said, "one giant leap for mankind." The astronauts found they had little difficulty walking on the moon where they spent over two hours collecting soil and rock samples. Before departing, they left behind an American flag. They splashed down in the Pacific Ocean on July 24, 1969.

The final U.S. mission to the moon was Apollo 17, which entered lunar orbit on December 10, 1972. The astronauts commemorated the culmination of the moon program by unveiling a plaque. Beneath drawings of Earth's two hemispheres and a central moon map, the text read, "Here man completed his first explorations of the Moon December 1972 A.D. May the spirit of peace in which we came be reflected in the lives of all mankind."

RIGHT: *Astronaut Edwin E. "Buzz" Aldrin, Jr., stands next to a solar wind experiment on the moon's pocked surface during the Apollo 11 mission.*

MISBEHAVING *in* AMERICA

The Watergate Scandal

It's been called "the most scandalous constitutional crisis in American history," but it began with "a third-rate burglary attempt." Five men were arrested early on the morning of June 17, 1972, inside the Democratic Party's national headquarters in the Watergate office complex in Washington, D.C. These were no ordinary burglars. They were carrying cameras and electronic surveillance gear and clearly were attempting to bug the offices.

One of the men, Jim McCord, Jr., was a former CIA employee who worked for President Richard Nixon's Committee to Re-elect the President (CRP, also called CREEP by Nixon's opponents). Documents found on the burglars led investigators to G. Gordon Liddy and E. Howard Hunt, who engineered the break-in. They were tried, along with the original five burglars, and convicted early in 1973 of conspiracy, burglary, and eavesdropping. After his

conviction, McCord charged that the White House and high Republican Party officials knew about the break-in, were covering up its connection to the crime, and had pressured the defendents to plead guilty to deflect attention from the Nixon Administration. His most startling claim, however, was that John N. Mitchell, former U.S. Attorney General in the Nixon Administration, had sanctioned the break-in. In response to McCord's allegations, Nixon opened an investigation of the burglary and his staff's involvement. Several key members of his adminstration resigned, but President Nixon vehemently denied any personal knowledge of a cover-up.

The media continued to investigate the scandal to assess how much the Nixon Administration knew about the break-in. Two reporters from the *Washington Post,* Bob Woodward and Carl Bernstein, doggedly pursued the story. They would cover the Watergate scandal (as it had come to be known) for two years. Known as Deep Throat, a top-secret source from within the government fed the two reporters tips and leads to help them in their research. They traced the origins of the scandal to the Justice Department and to the White House itself.

WHO WAS DEEP THROAT?

The mysterious character played by Hal Holbrook in *All the President's Men* (1976) was a man in the shadows, the cigarette-smoking source who helped *Washington Post* reporters Bob Woodward and Carl Bernstein bring down the Nixon Administration. For years, Holbrook's portrayal was the closest anyone got to Deep Throat's identity. Woodward and Bernstein zealously guarded their source's identity. In the years following the scandal, guessing who Deep Throat was became a popular pastime; some even speculated that there never was a Deep Throat, that he was just a fabrication. But in May 2005, Bob Woodward ended the mystery and confirmed that Deep Throat was W. Mark Felt, former deputy associate director of the Federal Bureau of Investigation during the Nixon Administration. ∎

In May 1973, a Senate committee headed by Senator Samuel J. Ervin, Jr., began televised hearings on the matter. White House Counsel John Dean delivered some of the most condemning testimony directly against Nixon. He gave detailed testimony about how White House officials, including Nixon, had colluded to cover up their role in the break-in.

Another former aide, Alexander Butterfield, testified that Nixon had tape recorded all his conversations in the White House since 1971. These tapes could have contained conversations Nixon had about the Watergate scandal and revealed exactly what he knew and when he knew it. The Senate committee subpoenaed the recordings.

Nixon fought the release of his tapes by claiming that they contained information vital to national security. While defending himself, he made his infamous pronouncement "I am not a crook." As a compromise, he agreed to release edited transcripts of the tapes that screened out top secret information.

The question of access to the tapes went all the way to the Supreme Court in *United States v. Nixon.* On July 24, 1974, the Court decided that Nixon's claims to executive privelege were void and ordered the tapes' surrender. When played, the tapes largely confirmed John Dean's version of events. There was also a blank portion of tape lasting about 18 and a half minutes. Nixon's secretary, Rose Mary Woods, claimed that she had accidentally erased portions, but there are many who believe the deletions were deliberate.

In the end, several high-up White House officials served time in prison on various convictions. Nixon, on the verge of impeachment, announced his resignation on August 8, 1974. He was pardoned, somewhat controversially, by his successor, Gerald R. Ford.

OPPOSITE: *Departing in disgrace, President Richard M. Nixon boards a helicopter to begin the journey to his new home in California on August 9, 1974, having resigned the presidency over the Watergate scandal. His was the first presidential resignation in American history.*

The NEW GLOBAL TENSIONS

Cold War and Iron Curtain

The peace at the end of World War II was relatively short-lived. An uneasy relationship grew between former allies the United States and the Soviet Union and their respective allies.

Within a few years of war's end, the Soviet Union was deeply involved in those countries of eastern Europe that its army had liberated: Communist governments were put in place. By 1950 Poland, Czechoslovakia, Bulgaria, Romania, and Hungary had communist governments taking orders from Moscow. Occupied Germany split into two nations, communist East Germany and democratic West Germany.

Under President Truman, the U.S. fought back with money and aid: The Marshall Plan, named for Secretary of State George C. Marshall, lent billions of dollars to countries of Western Europe, solidifying their allegiance to the U.S. In June 1948 the Soviet Union cut off all land traffic into the zones of Berlin occupied by the Western allies. The allies responded with an airlift, delivering food and supplies to stranded Berliners. After 11 months the Soviet Union ended its blockade. In 1949 the U.S. and 11 other countries formed the North Atlantic Treaty Organization (NATO) to protect one another from communist aggression. The Soviet Union and its allies formed the Warsaw Pact.

In 1949, the Soviets exploded their first atomic warhead, ending the U.S. monopoly on the weapon, and communists came to power in mainland China. The balance of power seemed more precarious. The Korean War brought the two superpowers into direct conflict. In 1961 the Soviets built a wall across Berlin to protect East Berliners from the West and stop the steady outward flow of German refugees fleeing westward.

In 1952 and 1953 both nations successfully tested a hydrogen bomb, a vastly more powerful nuclear weapon. They also began developing ballistic missiles that could deliver the weapons across continents and oceans. In 1962 the Soviets began secretly installing the missiles in Cuba, just 90 miles from American shores, resulting in the Cuban Missile Crisis. President Kennedy ordered a naval blockade, threatening to stop and board any Soviet ship trying to bring weapons. With Russian freighters nearing the blockade line, Premier Nikita Khrushchev backed down and ordered the missiles removed.

Throughout the Cold War, both went to pains to avoid military confrontation, choosing to resort to combat operations only to stop allies from defecting or to overthrow them after they had done so. Soviets troops preserved communist rule in East Germany in 1953, Hungary in 1956, Czechoslovakia in 1968, and Afghanistan in 1979. The U.S. helped overthrow a government in Guatemala in 1954, staged an unsuccessful invasion of Cuba in 1961, invaded the Dominican Republic in

NIXON IN CHINA

One of Richard Nixon's first acts as president was to dictate on February 1, 1969, a memo to his National Security Adviser, Henry Kissinger, urging him to explore the possibility of opening a diplomatic door to Communist China. Nearly two years later, Kissinger flew to China for a secret meeting with Chinese Prime Minister Zhou Enlai. After his visit, On July 11 he cabled Nixon one word: "Eureka!" A few days later Nixon announced Kissinger's trip and his acceptance of an invitation to visit Beijing.

Nixon expected to widen the growing breach between China and the Soviet Union. Nixon was taking a great risk. At home he might alienate the Republican right wing and especially friends of Taiwan in Congress. He flew to China without an appointment with Chairman Mao Zedong, who was bedridden, and he might have been publicly rebuffed. But Mao dragged himself from bed and met with Nixon. The meeting tipped the balance of power toward the West nor did it lose Taiwan; Nixon was correct that China would not risk the new American friendship to attack the island.

The trip has been called Nixon's finest hour. ■

1965 and Grenada in 1983, and undertook to prevent communist North Vietnam from over-running South.

In the 1960s and 1970s, the world became more subtly complicated. A split occurred between the Soviet Union and China, shattering the unity of the communist bloc. Western Europe and Japan emerged as economic forces. With the Stategic Arms Limitation Treaties (SALT), the two superpowers set limits on missile systems, though they continued massive arms buildups. With the arrival of Soviet Leader Mikhail S. Gorbachev and his reforms in the late 1980s, the Soviet Union's days were numbered. In late 1991 it collapsed altogether, and the Cold War came to an end.

OPPOSITE: *Painted in 1952, Chinese communist leader Mao Zedong stands in front of a red flag painted with portraits of Stalin, Lenin, Engels, and Marx.*

ABOVE: *Graffiti adorns the now toppled west side of the Berlin Wall. A glimpse of East Germany can be seen through the small slit.*

The GULF WAR

Operation Desert Storm

"Fight them with your faith in God, fight them in defense of every free honorable woman and every innocent child, and in defense of the values of manhood and the military honor . . . Fight them because with their defeat you will be at the last entrance of the conquest of all conquests. The war will end with . . . dignity, glory, and triumph for your people, army, and nation." Saddam Hussein, addressing his people on the radio on January 19, 1991, rallied them to oppose the coming invasion by America. The Gulf War, fought during 1990 and 1991, began when Iraq invaded Kuwait on August 2, 1990. Iraq was attempting to expand its power in the Gulf region, to void a large debt that Iraq owed Kuwait, and to control Kuwait's oil reserves.

The United Nations Security Council called for Iraq to withdraw and imposed a worldwide ban on trade with the nation. The invasion was a threat to Saudi Arabia, the world's largest oil producer and exporter; the U.S. and its Western European NATO allies rushed troops to deter a possible attack. The military buildup was called Operation Desert Shield. President George Bush issued an ultimatum to Saddam Hussein. "A line has been drawn in the sand.... Withdraw from Kuwait unconditionally and immediately, or face the terrible consequences."

On November 29, 1990, the UN Security Council authorized the use of force against Iraq. An allied coalition responded, and by January 1991, 700,000 troops, including 550,000 from the U.S. and lesser numbers from Britain, France, Egypt, Saudi Arabia, Syria, and several other countries, were assembled there.

The fighting began on January 16, 1991. Four-star General H. Norman Schwarzkopf addressed his troops: "I have seen in your eyes a fire of determination to get this war job done quickly. My confidence in you is total, our cause is just. Now you must be the thunder and lightning of Desert Storm."

President Bush spoke to the nation that night: "As I report to you, air attacks are under way against military targets in Iraq . . . Our troops will have the best possible support in the entire world, and they will not be asked to fight with one hand tied behind their back." Called Operation Desert Storm, the attack on Iraq began with sustained aerial bombardment, which smashed bridges, roads, refineries, munitions plants, buildings, and communications networks. Several weeks before Baghdad was bombed, U.S.

COLIN POWELL

The son of Jamaican immigrants who settled in New York City, Colin Powell found his calling in the Reserve Officers Training Corps in college. He served with distinction in several posts around the world, including two tours in Vietnam, where he was wounded, and rose quickly through the Army's ranks. When President George H. W. Bush named him to lead the Joint Chiefs of Staff in 1989, he was, at 52, the youngest man and the first African American ever to attain the country's highest military office. Just months into his tenure he led the intervention that ousted Panama dictator Manuel Noriega. When U.S. officials called for interventions, or shows of force, around the world, Powell urged caution: such movement of troops as a signal was too often an attempt "to give the appearance of clarity to mud."

In his autobiography, My American Journey, he writes: "Many of my generation, . . . seasoned in that war [Vietnam] vowed that when our turn came to call the shots, we would not quietly acquiesce in halfhearted warfare for half-baked reasons that the American people could not understand or support." ∎

intelligence had successfully inserted a virus into Iraq's military computers, disabling much of the air-defense system; bombing destroyed the rest. By mid-February Iraq's forward troops in Kuwait and southern Iraq were the target of bombers.

On February 24, Operation Desert Sabre, a ground offensive, moved out of Saudi Arabia into Kuwait and southern Iraq, and within three days retook Kuwait City. In the meantime, 120 miles west of Kuwait, Saddam's armored reserves were being attacked from the rear by U.S. tanks. By February 27, most of Iraq's elite Republican Guard units had been destroyed, and by February 28 Iraqi resistance had collapsed. President Bush declared a cease-fire.

An attempt was made on Saddam Hussein's life on the final night of the war. Just before the cease-fire, two U.S. Air Force bombers attacked a bunker 15 miles northwest of Baghdad where Saddam was thought to be. Two 5,000-pound bombs destroyed it, but Saddam was not killed.

The U.S. and its allies lost 300 troops in the conflict, but an estimated 60,000 Iraqi soldiers were killed. Lieutenant General Tom Kelly said,

"Iraq went from the fourth-largest army in the world to the second-largest army in Iraq in 100 hours." As many as a quarter of the Americans who were killed died from so-called friendly fire.

The defeated Hussein agreed to destroy his weapons of mass destruction—nuclear, biological, and chemical—and recognized Kuwait's sovereignty. Economic sanctions against Iraq continued until compliance was assured. When Iraq failed to cooperate with UN weapons inspectors in 1998, Operation Desert Fox caused a resumption of fighting. With Saddam defeated, northern Kurds and southern Shi'ites rose up in rebellion but were suppressed. "No-fly" zones were created over their regions to provide some protection.

ABOVE: *Like creatures from another world, environmentalists in protective suits examine the tar-encrusted ground amid raging oil fires in Kuwait. Iraq's 1990 invasion of its neighbor led to widespread damage to the country's oilfields.*

NEXT: *A U.S. Air Force 5-15 Eagle refuels for a mission over Iraq to enforce the United Nations no-fly zone.*

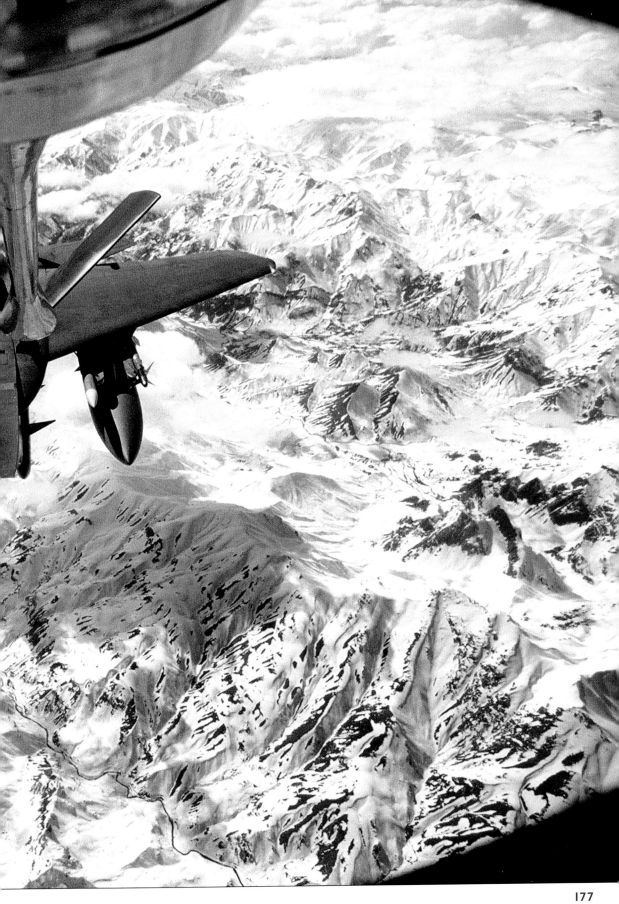

ATTACKS *on* AMERICA

Terrorism at Home

Isolated by surrounding oceans and insulated by complacency, America had felt safe from acts of terrorism. That ended when internal and external extremists came to threaten the nation in 1995 and 2001.

A massive, smoky explosion on April 19, 1995, ripped through the entire front of the Alfred P. Murrah Federal Building in Oklahoma City, Oklahoma. At the time, the blast was the worst terrorist attack in U.S. history; it killed 169 people and injured 850 more. Right-wing extremist Timothy McVeigh and his partner Terry Nichols drove a Ryder truck loaded with explosives into the building. McVeigh lit a timed fuse and walked away, before the bomb detonated and destroyed the northern half of the building.

Their target housed mostly government offices—welfare and social security. Most importantly, it held the regional offices of the federal Bureau of Alcohol, Tobacco, and Firearms, the place from which agents, in 1993, had been sent to take part in the 51-day standoff at the Branch Davidian headquarters in Waco, Texas. Roughly 80 Branch Davidians died when federal officials raided their headquarters. McVeigh believed that his actions were justified as retaliation for the events at Waco.

The date he chose for the attack—April 19—was important to him, an anniversary of several events: Patriot's Day in New England, the day the American Revolution had begun in 1775; the day in 1943 that the Nazis had moved on the Warsaw ghetto to destroy the city's Jewish population;

and the day in 1993 when the Branch Davidian compound burned to the ground.

On June 11, 2001, McVeigh, convicted of planting the bomb, was put to death in Terre Haute, Indiana, the first federal prisoner to be executed since 1963. He was led to his execution unrepentant. In an interview with the Sunday *Times* of London, he said, "When they [the government] govern by the sword, they must reckon with protest by the sword."

America faced its deadliest foreign terrorist attack on September 11, 2001. A team of hijackers operating under the direction of the wealthy son of a Saudi Arabian businessman, Osama bin Laden, commandeered commercial jetliners and flew them into targets in New York and Washington, D.C.

The first plane, a Boeing 767, struck the North Tower of the World Trade Center in New York City just before 9:00 a.m., as the city was beginning a work day. A few minutes later a second plane struck the South Tower. Both planes exploded into fireballs that ignited the top floors of the two towers. Then, as America watched transfixed, the horror grew worse: Within a mushrooming cloud of gray dust and smoke, the South Tower collapsed upon itself. A billowing mass of dust, smoke, and debris spread through the canyon-like streets of lower Manhattan. Half an hour later the North Tower also collapsed. Fires, fueled by the 10,000 gallons of jet fuel that each plane carried, had heated steel girders up to 2,000°F, softening them to the point where they could no longer support their great weight.

Meanwhile, at 9:40 a.m., a third hijacked plane en route from Washington, D.C., to Los Angeles dove like a missile into one side of the Pentagon in Arlington, Virginia, across the Potomac River from Washington, D.C. In rural Pennsylvania, another hijacked plane, whose passengers had learned from conversations on their cell phones what was happening, fought back against the hijackers. Their plane crashed into an empty field. Its intended target had evidently been either the White House or the U.S. Capitol.

The attackers, most of whom were soon identified, were filled with religious conviction, hatred of secular society, and the determination to demonstrate power through acts of violence. America is often a trading partner and political ally of regimes around the world that are regarded by their religious opponents as primary foes. In an increasingly small world, the cultural image that America projects, through MTV, Hollywood movies, and the Internet, is seen as a threat in fundamentalist Islamic cultures. Even multinational corporations are thought to be primarily American in attitude. Self-destructive violence, the hijackers believed, assured them of an immediate martyrdom and eternal bliss in heaven. With the finger of blame pointing to bin Laden, American and British warplanes on October 7, 2001, attacked Afghanistan, bringing down the Taliban regime that had protected and supported him. The Taliban were soon defeated, and bin Laden and his Al Qaeda cohorts went into hiding in the desolate mountains along the Afghanistan border with Pakistan.

OPPOSITE: *A gaping hole appears in the side of the Pentagon, one day after the terrorist attacks of September 11, 2001, that killed 184 people in Arlington, Virginia.* BELOW: *The grounds of the World Trade Center continue to smolder 15 days after a pair of airplanes struck the North and South Towers, causing them to collapse. In New York, roughly 2,750 people were killed on September 11.*

A SECOND WAR
in the GULF

~

Operation Iraqi Freedom

Rumblings of a second war in Iraq began shortly after the attacks of September 11, 2001. President George W. Bush argued that the attacks had exposed America's vulnerability to outside threats and that measures needed to be taken to protect the country.

In January 2002 President George W. Bush labeled Iraq a part of an "axis of evil." He insisted that the world must confront the "grave and gathering danger" of Iraq. Suspicions emerged that Iraq was developing weapons of mass destruction—chemical, biological, and nuclear.

Although these suspicions were later proved to be unsubstantiated, at the time U.S. leaders expressed the fear that these weapons could be used against enemies in the Gulf or traded to terrorists. President George W. Bush issued an ultimatum to the Iraqi dictator: Allow United Nations weapons inspectors back into Iraq or suffer the consequences.

On November 27, 2002, a weapons inspection team from the United Nations returned to Iraq. They did not turn up any weapons, but U.S. officials maintained that Hussein did have a

stockpile of dangerous weapons. U.S. Secretary of State Colin Powell went before the UN Security Council several times in February 2003 to convince the 15-member group that only military action could stop Saddam Hussein from hiding weapons of mass destruction. President Bush gave Hussein 48 hours to leave Iraq.

The world at large was not in favor of invading Iraq. In February 2003 protests against a possible war with Iraq took place in more than 350 cities worldwide. Some of America's allies, including France, Germany, and Russia, opposed an attack on Iraq without an authorizing resolution from the United Nations. French President Jacques Chirac said, "We are no longer in an era where one or two countries can control the fate of another country." But more than 40 countries around the world announced their support for the use of force against Iraq.

SADDAM HUSSEIN

The son of poor farmers, Saddam Hussein grew up in a village of mud-brick huts called Al-ouja. An uncle who was an army officer and crusader for Arab unity inspired him to go into politics.

He joined the socialist Ba'ath party at 19 and made his mark three years later by participating in a 1959 assassination attempt against Iraq's Prime Minister, Abdul Karim Qasim. Saddam was wounded in the leg during the failed effort and fled the country.

In 1963 he returned to Iraq and helped lead the revolt in 1968, under Gen. Ahmed Hassan al-Bakr, that brought the Ba'ath Party to power. He was made vice president of the country and built an elaborate network of secret police to suppress dissidents. Eleven years later he deposed Bakr and made himself president.

He allowed no dissenting voices to be raised and killed dozens of government officials he suspected of disloyalty. In the 1980s he resorted to chemical weapons to crush a Kurdish rebellion, brutally killing thousands of people.

In 1980 Saddam invaded Iran, starting an eight-year war that ended in stalemate. And in August 1990 he invaded Kuwait, defying UN directives to withdraw and provoking what he called "the mother of all battles." ■

Two hours after the expiration of the deadline, the U.S. and its allies launched Operation Iraqi Freedom. On March 19, 2003, forces consisting of 40 cruise missiles and strikes by two F-117s from the 8th Fighter Squadron and other aircraft attacked. President Bush addressed the American public, announcing that coalition forces were in the "early stages of military operations to disarm Iraq, to free its people, and to defend the world from grave danger."

This first phase of the war was relatively short. From March to April 2003, the combined military efforts of the U.S., Great Britain, and other nations quickly defeated the conventional military forces of Iraq. Operation Iraqi Freedom was the biggest military operation mounted since the Vietnam War. On May 2, aboard the U.S.S. *Lincoln*, President Bush proudly proclaimed that military operations had ceased and that securing and reconstructing the country would begin.

Saddam Hussein himself was captured on December 13, 2003, in a remote farmhouse near Tikrit. He was turned over to Iraqi authorities in 2004 and tried for crimes against humanity in 2006. Found guilty, Hussein was executed on December 30, 2006.

Rebuilding Iraq has proved more difficult than the initial military campaign. To assist the fledgling government in providing security for its people, American armed forces have occupied Iraqi cities. Their presence has been violently opposed by an armed insurgency that has staged numerous bloody attacks on both Iraqis and Americans. Support for the war among American citizens has waned since 2003. In November 2006, Democratic control of Congress returned, as voters expressed their displeasure with the war. Since 2003, more than 3,400 Americans have lost their lives in the conflict.

OPPOSITE: *In April 2007, an Iraqi soldier searches for weapons in a joint assault with U.S. Army forces.*
NEXT: *An Iraqi woman waits for the start of fuel distribution during a humanitarian visit in 2007. More than 5,000 gallons of diesel fuel and 525 canisters of kerosene were distributed by U.S. Army soldiers.*

AMERICANS EXPLORE

Flying Higher, Going Deeper

Dr. Sylvia Earle allowed herself to be bolted into Jim, a cumbersome pressurized diving suit. A small submarine descended with her to a depth of 1,250 feet off the island of Oahu. Once on the ocean bottom, she unhooked herself from the sub and set off to explore. With no connection to the surface, and only a thin communications line attaching her to the sub, she wandered alone for two and a half hours.

Her solo expedition to the seafloor in 1979 would change the space explorer profile forever: It led directly to the first class of women entering the U.S. astronaut training program. Earle had proven that women have the endurance needed for space exploration. And with Sally Ride they began to man a new NASA brainchild: the space shuttle.

In January 1972 the Apollo moon program was coming to an end, even though there were two lunar landings yet to come. NASA looked around for new projects and settled upon a space shuttle, a reusable craft that would lift off like a rocket, carry people and cargo into Earth's orbit, then land on a runway like an airplane. After servicing, it would be ready to fly again. President Nixon said, "I have decided today that the United States should proceed at once with the development of an entirely new type of space transportation system designed to help transform the space frontier of the 1970s into familiar territory, easily accessible for human endeavor in the 1980s and 1990s." The space shuttle was meant to make space flight routine, all while carrying 65,000 pounds of cargo and seven people.

On January 28, 1986, the shuttle program faced its first tragedy when the *Challenger* exploded and took the lives of its seven crew members, including Christa McAuliffe, a school teacher who had been selected as the first private citizen to fly on the craft. Almost 20 years later, another shuttle tragedy would remind the country of the dangers inherent in space exploration: The shuttle *Columbia* would break apart when returning from a mission on February 1, 2003.

One of the shuttle's most important accomplishments was the launching and repair of the Hubble Space Telescope. On April 24, 1990, the NASA announcer intoned, ". . . and liftoff of the space shuttle *Discovery* with the Hubble Space Telescope—our window on the universe." But the window was foggy.

NASA scientists discovered that the telescope's vision was flawed—its primary mirror was 2.5 millionths of a meter too flat at the edge. Images sent back to earth had a smudge or blur in the center of each image. The telescope couldn't be brought back to earth, so repair had to be done in space. A highly experienced crew of seven astronauts set off on December 2, 1993, to fix

Hubble. They installed a package to correct the flaw in the mirror, as well as replaced two gyroscopes that had worn out, removed Hubble's damaged solar arrays and replaced them with new ones, and installed a new wide-field camera. By 1993 Hubble had looked deeper into the universe than ever had been done before, revealing thousands of galaxies and allowing astronomers to trace the evolution of the universe. In its first ten years, Hubble snapped 330,000 exposures and focused on 14,000 targets in space.

Twenty-first-century exploration has incorporated robotic technology to augment human voyages. Latest in a long line of robotic explorers in space, NASA's Opportunity and Spirit were scuttling around on the surface of Mars in early 2004, photographing and gathering readings on Martian minerals. Their primary mission was to look for evidence that Mars was once warmer and wetter than it is today. In February, Spirit, using a diamond-tipped abrasion tool spinning 3,000 times a minute, ground into a rock termed Adirondack, allowing scientists to get their first look at pristine minerals.

OPPOSITE: *Dangling beneath a minisub, Dr. Sylvia Earle ascends to the surface following a solo stroll on the seafloor in 1979. At a depth of 1,250 feet she performed a two-and-a-half-hour exploration. Earle's walk proved the dexterity of women and was a direct precursor to women being accepted into the U.S. space program.*

ABOVE: *Anchored only by his feet during this 6-hour, 44-minute space walk, Astronaut James S. Voss snaps pictures with a 35 mm camera from the outside of the Space Shuttle* Atlantis *in 2000. Voss and his fellow astronauts made significant repairs to the International Space Station, including improvements to the communications systems.*

INDEX

~

Boldface indicates illustrations.

A

Abernathy, Ralph 160
Abilene, Kansas 92
Abolitionists 24, 76–77, 84
Ada County, Idaho 94
Adams, Henry 112
Adams, John 29, 35, 36, **38**, 41
Adams, Samuel 29
Addams, Jane 122
Adirondack Mountains, New York 101
Afghanistan 181
Africa: slave trade 24, 26
African Americans: civil rights movement 156–57, 159, 160, 161; labor unions 99; Reconstruction 86, 87, 156; World War I 119, 156; *see also* Slavery
Airplanes 79, 108, **109–11**, 119
Alabama 26, 87
Alamo, San Antonio, Texas **64**, 65, **66–67**
Alamogordo, New Mexico 148
Alaska 10
Albany, New York 19, 52
Albemarle Sound, North Carolina 31
Alcatraz Island, San Francisco Bay, California 141
Aldrich, Thomas Bailey 130
Aldrin, Edwin E. "Buzz," Jr. 168, **169**
Alexandria, Virginia 26
Allegheny Mountains 52
Allen, Steve 152
Allen, Woody 152
Al Qaeda 181
Amazon.com 179
American Anti-Slavery Society 84
American Federation of Labor (AFL) 99
American Indian Movement 141
American Red Cross 99
American Revolution 29, 31, 34, **35, 36,** 37, 40
American River, California 72
Anasazi 11
Anders, William 168
Angel Island Immigration Station, San Francisco Bay, California 131
Anglicans 21
Anthony, Susan B. 122, 123
Antietam, Battle of 81
Apache 140
Apollo program 167, **168–69**, 186
Appleton, Nathan 55
Archer, William 151
Arkansas 87
Arkansas River 52
Armour, Philip 72–73
Armstrong, Louis **135**
Armstrong, Neil 168
Arnaz, Desi **153**
Articles of Confederation 37, 40
Ashley, William 56
Associated Press 104
Astor, John Jacob 97
AT&T 105, 134, 152
Atlanta, Georgia 83, 88
Austin, Stephen 62
Austin, Texas 62
Austinville, Virginia 62
Austria-Hungary 118
Automobiles 114, 115, **116–17**

B

Bacon, Robert 96

Bainbridge, Kenneth T. 148
Balboa, Vasco Núñez de 16, 18
Ball, Lucille **153**
Baltimore, Maryland 132
Baltimore and Ohio Railroad 88, 98
Baptists 21
Barton, Clara 99
Bastro, Luis Cancer de 20
Bean, Phantly "Roy" 94
Bell, Alexander Graham 104, **105**
Bell, Rex 127
Bell Telephone Company 104
Bennett, Hugh Hammond 137
Berle, Milton 152
Berlin, Germany 145, 172
Berlin Wall 172, **173**
Bernstein, Carl 171
Bessemer, Henry 96
Bibb, Henry 76
Bill of Rights 6, 21, 40
Billy the Kid 94
Bin Laden, Osama 180, 181
Bitterroot Mountains, Montana–Idaho 51
Black, Martin 134
Block, Martin 134
Booth, John Wilkes 83
Borman, Frank 168
Boston, Massachusetts 34, 35, 36, 132, 163
Boston Massacre **35**
Boston Tea Party 34
Bow, Clara **126**, 127
Bowie, James "Jim" 65
Bozeman Trail 140
Brannan, Sam 72
Branch Davidians 180
Bridger, Jim 100
Brin, Sergey 179
Brooklyn Museum, Brooklyn, New York 5
Brooks, Mel 152
Brotherhood of Sleeping Car Porters 99
Brown, Henry "Box" 76
Brown, John 76
Brown, Moses 54
Brown University, Providence, Rhode Island 21
Brown v. Board of Education 156, 157
Buffalo, New York 52
Bulge, Battle of 145
Bull Run, First Battle of 80, 99
Bunker Hill, Battle of 36
Bureau of Alcohol, Tobacco, and Firearms 180
Bureau of Indian Affairs 141
Bureau of Refugees, Freedmen, and Abandoned Lands 87
Burnett, John G. 61
Burr, Aaron 40, 41
Bush, George H. W. 174
Bush, George W. 182, 183
Bushnell, David 34
Butterfield, Alexander 171

C

Cabot, John 16, 18
Cabral, Pedro Alvares 16
Caesar, Sid 152
Cahokia (site), Illinois 11
California: Civil War 79; gold rush 72–73, 79; immigration 56; missions 21; railroads 88; statehood 80; surrender by Mexico 62
Calvert, Leonard 31
Canada 76–77, 133
Canals 52
Cape Cod, Massachusetts 19
Cape of Good Hope, South Africa 16
Capra, Frank 127
Carnegie, Andrew 96, 97

Carson, Kit 56
Cartier, Jacques 18
Casa Grande Ruin, Arizona 11
Cather, Willa 69
Catlin, George 100
Centennial Exposition of 1876 98, 104
Central Pacific Railroad 88, 89
Centreville, Virginia **82**, 83
Chaco Canyon, New Mexico 11
Champlain, Samuel de 18
Chaplin, Charlie 126, 127
Charles, Ray 152
Charles II, King (England) 30
Chattanooga, Tennessee 88
Cherokees 60, **61**, 71
Chesapeake Bay 18
Chicago, Illinois: immigrants 132; riots 98; stockyards 92, 112
Child labor 112, **113**, 122
China: immigrants from 131, 133; Korean War 155; Nixon's visit 173; World War II 144
Chirac, Jacques 183
Chisholm Trail 92
Chrysler, Walter P. 115
Chrysler Corporation 115
Cincinnati, Ohio 77, 88
Civilian Conservation Corps (CCC) 138, **139**
Civil Rights Acts 6, 159
Civil rights movement 156–57, 159, 160, 161
Civil War (1861–1865) **80–82**, 83, 84, 88, 99
Clark, William 48–49, 51
Clay, Henry 68
Cleveland, Ohio 132
Coal 96
Coca, Imogene 152
Cody, William Frederick "Buffalo Bill" 94, **95**
Coffin, Levi and Catherine 77
Cold War 172–73
Coleridge, Samuel Taylor 75
Collier, John 141
Colonial period 18–19, 30–31, 34–38
Colorado 73, 122
Colorado River 101, **102–3**
Columbia River 46, 51
Columbus, Christopher 9, 16, 17
Communism 154, 162, 172–73
Como, Perry 152
Compromise of 1850 80
Concord, Massachusetts 36
Confederacy 80–83, 86
Congress of Industrial Organizations (CIO) 99
Congress of Racial Equality (CORE) 157
Connecticut 30, 31, 45
Constitution *see* U.S. Constitution
Cook, James 10
Coolidge, Calvin 134
Cooper, James Fenimore 57
Córdoba, Francisco Fernández de 16
Cornwallis, Charles 37
Coronado, Francisco Vásquez de 18
Côrte-Real, Gaspar 16
Cortés, Hernán 17, 18
Cotton 42–43, **54**, 84
Cowboys **92**, 93
Creek Indians 60
Crockett, Davy 65, **66**
Cronkite, Walter 160
Cuba 16, 99, 132, 172
Cuban Missile Crisis 172
Currency 30
Currier, Charles 88
Custer, George 141

D

Da Gama, Vasco **16**, 17
Dallas, Texas 153, 160

Daniels, Jonathan 144
Davis, Jefferson 80, 83
Dawes Act of 1887 141
Dayton, Ohio 88, 108
D-Day **106–7**
Dean, John 171
Declaration of Independence 6, 36, **38–39**
De Forest, Lee 134
Delany, Martin 84
Delaware 31
DeMille, Cecil B. 126
Democratic Party 83, 156, 170, 183
Democratic-Republicans 40–41
Denmark: immigrants from 132
De Soto, Hernando 18
D'Estaing, Jean Baptiste 37
D'Estaing, Valéry Giscard 151
Detroit, Michigan 114, 157
Díaz, Bernal 17
Dickinson, John 38
Dodge brothers 114, 115
Douglass, Frederick 84
Dulles, John Foster 162
Dunlap, John 38
Dunne, Finley Peter 112
Durant, William 114
Durham, North Carolina **158–59**
Dust Bowl 137

E

Earhart, Amelia 109
Earle, Sylvia **186**, 187
Earp, Virgil 94
East St. Louis, Illinois 92
eBay 179
Edwards, Jonathan 21, 40
Einstein, Izzy 125
Eisenhower, Dwight David 116, 157, 162
Elizabeth I, Queen (England) 18
Ellington, Duke 136
Ellis, Samuel 130
Ellis Island, New York Harbor, New York **130–31**
Emancipation Proclamation 6, 81, 84
England: colonies 18–19, 24, 29, 30–31, 34–38; explorers 17, 18; immigrants from 133; railroads 88; textile industry 43; wars with France 29, 34, 37; World War I 118, 119
Enola Gay (airplane) 146, 148
Equiano, Olaudah 24
Ericksson, Leif 9, 12
Erie Canal, New York 52
Erik the Red 12
Ervin, Samuel J., Jr. 171
Evans, Harold 125, 162
Exploration: North America 12, 16–19, 56; seafloor **186**; space **166–69**, **186**, **187**

F

Fairbanks, Douglas 126
Fairfield, John 76
Fair Labor Standards Act of 1938 113
Fargo, William 73
Faulkner, William 127
Federal Arts Project (FAP) 138
Federal Fair Housing Law 159
Federalists 40–41
Federal Writers' Project (FWP) 138, 139
Felt, W. Mark 171
Ferdinand, Franz, Archduke 118
Fitzgerald, F. Scott 125, 127
Flemming, Victor 127
Florida 87
Floyd, Charles 49
Ford, Gerald 171
Ford, Henry 114, 115

Ford Motor Company 115
Ford's Theater, Washington, D.C. 83
Fort Laramie, Wyoming 140
Fort Mandan, North Dakota 49
France: explorers 17; Louisiana Purchase 46–47; settlements 18, 31, 46; wars with England 29, 34, 37; World War I 118, 119, 120–21; World War II 144–45
Franklin, Benjamin **38**
Free Soil Party 84
Fugitive Slave Act of 1850 76, 80
Fulton, Robert 43, 52
Fur trade 19, 46, 56

G

Gagarin, Yuri 166
Gage, Thomas 36
Galbraith, John Kenneth 137
Gallatin, Albert 52
Gast, John 71
Gelbart, Larry 152
Gemini program 167
General Grant National Memorial, New York, New York 100
General Motors 114–15
Geneva, Switzerland **178**, 179
Gennaro, Peter 152
George II, King (England) 31
George III, King (England) 36
Georgia: Civil War 82, 83; colonial period 31; Native Americans 60; readmission to Union 87
Georgia Railroad 88
Germany: Cold War 172; highway system 116; immigrants from 130; World War I 118–19, 121; World War II 144–45, 147
Gettysburg, Battle of 81
Gila River, New Mexico–Arizona 10
Glenn, John 166
Glidden, Joseph F. 93
Glyn, Elinor 127
Gold rush **72–73**
Goldwyn, Samuel 126
Gompers, Samuel 99
Google 179
Gorbachev, Mikhail S. 173
Gorgas, Josiah 81
Grand Canyon National Park, Arizona 101, **102–3**
Grand Central Station, New York, New York 89
Grant, Cary 127
Grant, Julia Dent 100
Grant, Ulysses S. **80**, 81–83, 87, 100
Great Awakening 21
Great Depression 115, 126, 137, 138
Great Northern Peninsula, Newfoundland, Canada 12
Great Smoky Mountains, Tennessee–North Carolina 61
Greece: immigrants from 133
Greeley, Horace 56
Greene, Catherine 42
Greene, Nathanael 37, 42
Greenland 10, 12, 16
Griffith, D. W. 126
Grimké, Sarah 84
Gros Morne National Park, Newfoundland, Canada 12, **14–15**
Guadalcanal Campaign 144
Guadeloupe Hidalgo, Treaty of (1848) 62
Gulf of Tonkin Resolution 162

H

Haiti, West Indies 16
Hall, John H. 55
Hamilton, Alexander 40, 41

Hammond, James Henry 42
Hancock, John 38
Harpers Ferry, West Virginia 48, 55, 82
Hartford, Connecticut 30
Hawaii 10, 133
Hawks, Howard 127
Hayes, Rutherford B. 87, 89
Henderson, Fletcher 136
Henrietta Maria, Queen (England) 31
Henry, Andrew 56
Henson, Josiah 26
Hepburn, Katharine 127
Highways 115–16
Hiroshima, Japan 146, 148
Hitchcock, Alfred 126
Hitler, Adolf 144, 145, 162
Hoffman, Abbie 165
Hohokam 10
Holbrook, Hal 171
Holland 17, 18, 30, 31
Holley, Alexander 96
Hollywood, California 126
Homestead Act of 1862 6, 68
Honolulu, Hawaii 133
Hoover, Herbert 137, 138
Hopkins, Harry 138
Hornaday, William Temple 101
Hough, Franklin B. 101
Houston, Sam 62, **63**
Howe, William 36
Howells, William Dean 98
Hubble Space Telescope 186–87
Hudson, Henry 18, 19
Hudson River, New York 17, 19
Hunt, E. Howard 170
Hussein, Saddam 174, 175, 182, 183
Hutchinson, Anne 21
Huxley, Aldous 127

I

Iceland 12
Idaho 73, 122
Immigration 130–33
Indianapolis, Indiana 88, 160
Indian Removal Act of 1830 60
Indian Reorganization Act of 1934 141
Indians *see* Native Americans
Industrial Revolution 54–55
Ingstad, Anne Stine and Helge 12
Intel Corporation 179
International Ladies' Garment Workers Union 99
International Red Cross 99, **119**
International Space Station 187
Internet 178–79
Inuit 10
Iran 183
Iraq 174–75, 182–83
Ireland: immigrants from 130, 132
Islam 161, 181
Italy: immigrants from 132, 133; World War I 118; World War II 144
Iwo Jima (island), Volcano Islands, Japan 145–46

J

Jackson, Andrew 60, 62, 68
James, Jesse and Frank 93–94
James River, Virginia 19, **74–75**
Jamestown, Virginia 19, 31
Japan: immigrants from 133; World War I 118; World War II 144–46, 147
Japanese Americans: internment camps 146
Jay, John 40
Jefferson, Thomas: Declaration of Independence **38**; Lewis and Clark Expedition 48, 51; Louisiana Purchase 46, 47; political party 40–41

Jews 132, 133
Jim Crow laws 156
Johnson, Andrew 83, 86
Johnson, Lyndon 162
Joseph (Nez Perce chief) 141
Junaluska (Cherokee chief) 60

K

Kamehameha, King (Hawaii) 10
Kansas 69
Kansas City, Missouri 92
Kansas Pacific Railroad 92
Karlsefni, Thorfinn Thorsdarrson 12
Kean, William B. **154**, 155
Kelley, Florence 122
Kelly, Tom 175
Kelly, William 96
Kennedy, Jacqueline 160
Kennedy, John F. 153, 160, **161**, 162, 172
Kennedy, Robert F. 160, 161
Kent State, Kent, Ohio 165
Kentucky 45, 123
Khrushchev, Nikita 172
King, Martin Luther, Jr. 159, 160, 161
Kipling, Rudyard 107
Kissinger, Henry 173
Kitty Hawk, North Carolina **109**
Knights of Labor 99
Korean War (1950-1953) **154**, 155
Ku Klux Klan 87
Kuwait 174, 175, 183

L

Labor unions 75, **98**, 99, 107
Land Ordinance of 1785 45
Lange, Dorothea 5
L'Anse aux Meadows (site), Newfoundland, Canada 12
Laramie, Wyoming 94
Lasky, Jessy 126
Leach, John A. **124**, 125
League of Nations 121
Lee, Ezra 34
Lee, Robert E. 80–83
Leland, Henry 114
Lenin, V. I. 119
Lewis, Jane 76
Lewis, John L. 99
Lewis, Meriwether 48–49, 51
Lewis and Clark Expedition 48–49; drawings **48**, 49, **50**, 51; map 49
Lexington, Massachusetts 36
Liddy, G. Gordon 170
Lincoln, Abraham: assassination 83; Civil War 76, **81**, 83; elections 80, 83; Emancipation Proclamation 81, 84; railroads 88; speeches 81, 83
Lincoln Highway 116
Lindbergh, Charles A. 108–9
Little Big Horn, Battle of 141
Little Rock, Arkansas 157
Livingston, Robert R. 38, 46, 47, 52
Lombardo, Guy 134
Londonderry, Ireland 109
Longfellow, Henry 37
Los Angeles, California 5, 157, 161
Louisiana 46, 87
Louisiana Purchase 40, 46, 47
Lovell, James 168
Lovell, Francis 55
Lucas, Stephen E. 38
Lynchings 156, **157**

M

MacArthur, Douglas **154**, 155
Magellan, Ferdinand 17
Mail service 78–79
Maine: prohibition law 125
Malcolm X **160**, 161
Mandan Indians 49

Manhattan, New York, New York 19, 30
Manhattan Project 148
Manifest Destiny 57, **70**, 71
Mannes, Marya 153
Manufacturing **54**, 55, 96–97, 112–13, 146–47
Mao Zedong **172**, 173
Maps: colonies 31; Lewis and Clark Expedition 49; lower Mississippi River 52; Tubac River 20; U.S. Steel 97; Washington, D.C. 41; Western Hemisphere 8–9
Marion, Indiana 157
Markham, Edwin 112
Marquises Islands 10
Mars 187
Marshall, George C. 172
Marshall, James 72
Marshall, John 40, 60
Marshall Plan 172
Marx Brothers 127
Maryland 21, 31
Massachusetts 30, 36, 37
Massachusetts Bay Colony 21, 30
Masterson, Bat 94
Matlack, Timothy 38
Maya 17
Mayflower Compact 30
McAuliffe, Christa 186
McClellan, George 83
McCord, Jim, Jr. 170–71
McCullough, David 108
McVeigh, Timothy 180
Meat Inspection Act of 1906 112
Memphis, Tennessee 86, 88, 160
Mennonites 21
Mercury program **166**, 167
Meridian, Mississippi 83
Mesa Verde National Park, Colorado 11
Meuse-Argonne Offensive 120–21
Mexican War (1846-1848) 62, **70**, 79
Mexico 62, 64–65, 70, 71, 118
Michigan: automobile industry 114
Midway, Battle of 144
Milwaukee, Wisconsin 132
Minuit, Peter 30
Missionaries 17, 20–21
Missions: San Antonio de Valero, Texas 20; San Diego de Alcala, California 21; San Juan Capistrano, California 21, **22–23**
Mississippi 26, 87
Mississippi River: Civil War 80, 81; early Native Americans 11; exploration 17; map 52; trade **44–45**, 52–53; tributaries 46
Missouri Indians 49
Missouri River 46, 48, 51, 52, 53
Mitchell, Charles 137
Mitchell, John 31, 171
Monroe, James 47
Montana 73
Montgomery, Alabama 157, 159
Moon landing 153, **168–69**
Moore, Annie 130
Moran, Percy 37
Morgan, J. P. 96, 97
Mormons 57, 69
Morris, Howard 152
Morrow, Edwin P. **123**
Morse, Samuel F. B. 79, 104
Mountbatten, Louis 126
Movies 126–29
Muhammad, Elijah 161
Muir, John 100, **101**
Muir Woods National Monument, California 100
Murrow, Edward R. 135, 152
Mystic Seaport, Connecticut 31, **32–33**

N

Nagasaki, Japan 146, 148, **149**
Napoleon Bonaparte 46, 47
National Aeronautics and Space Administration (NASA) 151, 166–67, 186–87
National Archives, Washington, D.C. 6, 38
National Association for the Advancement of Colored People (NAACP) 156, 157
National Consumer's League 122
National Industrial Recovery Act (NIRA) 138
National Origins Act of 1929 133
National parks 100–101
Native Americans: archaeological sites 11, 101; in art 4, 5; first European encounters 16, 17, 18; government policies 60–61, 140–41; language 60; Lewis and Clark Expedition 48–49, 51; pre-Columbian 9, 10–11; relationships with colonists 19, 29; religious conversion 20–21; reservations 141; Trail of Tears 60, **61**; westward expansion 71, 100
Navajo 140
Nevada 73
Newark, New Jersey 157
New Deal 138–39
New Echota, Treaty of (1835) 60
Newfoundland, Canada 12, 16
New Hampshire 30
New Haven, Connecticut 104
New Jersey 31
New Mexico 62
New Orleans, Louisiana: immigration 131; race riots 86; slavery 26; trade 46, 53; waterfront 44–**45**
Newport, Rhode Island 37
New York: colonial period 30–31; slavery 26; western boundary 45
New York, New York: Great Depression **136**, 137; immigrants **130**–32; parades **28–29**, 119; Prohibition 124, 125; strikes **98**, **99**; telephones **104**, 105; terrorist attacks 180, **181**; trade 52
Nez Percé Indians 51, 141
Nicholas II, Tsar (Russia) 118
Nichols, Terry 180
Nimitz, Chester W. 146
Nixon, Richard 153, 162, 165, **170**, 171, 173, 186
Noonan, Fred 109
Noriega, Manuel 174
Normandy, France **106–7**, 144
North, Simeon 55
North Atlantic Treaty Organization (NATO) 172
North Carolina 31, 87
Northern Pacific Railroad 89
Northfield, Minnesota 94
Norway: immigrants from 132
Nuclear weapons 146, 148, 172, 173

O

Oglethorpe, James 31
Ohio River 45, 76
Oklahoma 61, 69
Oklahoma City, Oklahoma: bombing 180
Olds, Ransom 114
Omaha, Nebraska 88, 92
Operation Desert Storm (Persian Gulf War) 174, **175–77**
Operation Iraqi Freedom 182–83
Oppenheimer, Robert 148
Oregon 56, 70
Oregon Trail 56–57, **58–59**
O'Sullivan, John 57, 70

Oswald, Lee Harvey 160
Otoe 49

P

Packard Motor Company **114**, 115
Page, Larry 179
Paine, Thomas 36
Painter, Nell Irvin 122
Panama, Isthmus of 16
Paris, France 109, 118, 121, 145, 165
Parks, Rosa 157
Paul, Alice 122
Pawtucket, Rhode Island 54
Peace Corps 151
Pearl Harbor, Oahu, Hawaii 144, **145**, 147
Pearson, Benjamin 76
Pedro II, Emperor (Brazil) 104
Penn, William 31
Pennsylvania 21, 31, 181
Pennsylvania Railroad 88
Pennsylvania Turnpike 116
Pentagon, Arlington, Virginia **180**, 181
Petersburg, Battle of 82, 83
Philadelphia, Pennsylvania 38, 98, 104, 132
Philippines 17
Pickford, Mary 126
Pilgrims 30
Pittsburgh, Pennsylvania 96, 98, 132
Pizarro, Francisco 17
Plessy v. Ferguson 156, 157
Pletcher, David M. 71
Plymouth Colony, Massachusetts 19, 30
Political parties 40–41, 84
Polk, James K. 62, 71, 72
Ponce de León, Juan 16, 18
Pony Express **78**, 79
Portsmouth, New Hampshire 30
Portsmouth, Rhode Island 21
Portugal: currency 30; explorers 16–17
Potomac River, Maryland 29
Powderly, Terence 99
Powell, Colin 174, 183
Preemption Act of 1841 68
Preminger, Otto 126
Presley, Elvis 152
Princeton University, Princeton, New Jersey 21
Progressive Party 122
Prohibition **124**, 125
Public Works Administration (PWA) 138
Pueblo Bonito, New Mexico 11
Pueblo Indians **140**, 141
Puerto Rico 16
Puget Sound, Washington 132
Pulaski, Tennessee 87
Pure Food and Drug Act of 1906 112
Puritans 21

Q

Quakers 21
Quebec, Canada 18
Quiroga, Miguel Angel González 71

R

Radio **134–35**
Railroads 79, 88, **89–91**, 98–99
Raleigh, Sir Walter 18
Randolph, A. Philip 99
Rankin, John 77
Ray, James Earl 160
Reconstruction 83, 86–87, 156
Red Cloud (Sioux chief) 140
Red River 72
Reiner, Carl 152
Religion 17, 20–21

Remington, Frederic 5, 79, 93
Republican Party 83, 84, 86–87, 156
Revere, Paul 35, 36, 37
Revolutionary War *see* American Revolution
Rhee, Syngman 154
Rhode Island 21, 30
Richmond, Virginia 74–**75**, 80, 81, 88
Ridgway, Matthew B. **154**, 155
Rio Grande, U.S.–Mexico 17, 18, 62
Roanoke Island, North Carolina 18–19
Robber barons 97
Robinson, Harriet 55
Rockefeller, John D. **96**, 97
Rockwell, Norman 145
Rocky Mountains 51
Rolfe, John 19, 24
Romania: immigrants from 133
Rome, New York 52
Roosevelt, Eleanor 122
Roosevelt, Franklin Delano: death 148; election 138; fireside chats 134; New Deal 138–39, 141; World War II 146, 147
Roosevelt, Theodore 7, 96, **101**, 109, 112, 122
Route 66 (highway) 115
Rubin, Jerry 165
Ruby, Jack 160
Rusk, Dean 154
Russia: immigrants from 133; revolution 118, 119; settlements 46; World War I 118, 119; *see also* Soviet Union

S

Sacagawea (Shoshone guide) 48, 51
Sacramento, California 78, 88
Saigon, South Vietnam 163
St. John de Crèvecoeur, Hector 75
St. Joseph, Missouri 78
St. Louis, Missouri 48, 51, 88, 108
Salt Lake City, Utah 132
Salt River, Arizona 10
San Antonio, Texas 64, 65
San Francisco, California 100, 105, 152, 155; gold rush 73; immigrants 132
San Gabriel, California 18
San Ildefonso, Treaty of (1800) 46
San Jacinto, Battle of 62, 65
San Juan Hill, Cuba 7
San Salvador (island), Bahamas, West Indies 16
Santa Anna, Antonio Lopez de 62, 64–65
Santo Domingo, Dominican Republic, West Indies 46–47
Saratoga, New York 37
Savannah, Georgia 42, 83
Schubert, Franz 57
Schwarzkopf, H. Norman 174
Scott, Dred 80
Scott, Winfield 80
Scovell, Bessie Laythe 124
Selective Service Act of 1917 119
Seoul, South Korea 154, 155
September 11 Terrorist Attacks, 2001 **180–81**
Sequoia National Park, California 100
Sequoyah (Cherokee chief) 60
Serbia: immigrants from 133; World War I 118
Seven Days' Battle 80
Shelly v. Kraemer 157
Shepard, Alan 166
Sherman, Roger 38
Sherman, William Tecumseh 69, 80, 82, 83

Sherman Anti-Trust Act of 1890 96
Shoshone 48
Siberia (region), Russia 10
Silicon Valley, California 179
Simon, Neil 152
Sinclair, Upton **112**, 113
Sioux 140, 141
Sirhan, Sirhan 161
Slater, Samuel 54
Slavery: abolitionist movement 24, 76–77, 84; beginning 9, 24; cotton plantations 42–43; Emancipation Proclamation 81, 84; laws 24; rebellions 24; ships 24, **25**; source of conflict 45, 80, 84; trade 24, 26; Underground Railroad 76, 77
Sloan, Alfred 114–15
Smith, Jedediah 56
Smith, John 18
Smith, Oliver 155
Smithsonian Institution, Washington, D.C. 101
Smith v. Allwright 156
Snake River 51
Social reform 112–13
Social Security 138
Soil Conservation Act of 1935 137
South Carolina: American Revolution 37; colonial period 31; railroads 88; readmission to Union 87; secession 80
Soviet Union 154, 166, 172–73
Space exploration 166–69, 186, 187
Space shuttle 186, **187**
Spain: currency 30; explorers 16–17; missionaries 17, 20–21; settlements 18, 31, 46
Spanish-American War (1898) 7, 99
Sputnik 166
Stalin, Joseph 146–47, 154
Stamp Act of 1765 34
Standard Oil 97
Stanford Research Park, Palo Alto, California 179
Statue of Liberty National Monument, New York Harbor, New York 133
Steamboats 52–53
Steel 96–97
Steiger, Rod 152
Stein, Gertrude 125
Steinbeck, John 115
Stevens, Thaddeus 83, 86
Stock market crash (1929) 136–37
Stono River, South Carolina 24
Stowe, Harriet Beecher 76, 77
Strategic Arms Limitation Treaties (SALT) 173
Strauss, Levi 72
Strikes 98, 99
Studebaker, John 73
Sugar Act of 1764 34
Sullivan, Ed 152
Sullivan, John 37
Sullivan's Island, Charleston 24, 26
Sumner, Charles 86
Sung, Kim Il 154–55
Sutter, John 72
Sweden: immigrants from 132

T

Tampa Bay, Florida 20
Telegraph 78, 79, 104
Telephone 104–5
Television **152–53**
Tennessee 87
Tennessee Valley Authority (TVA) 138
Terre Haute, Indiana 180
Terrorism 180–81
Tet Offensive 163
Texas 62–65, 71; readmission to Union 87; Revolution 62, 64–65

Textile mills 54, 55
Tilden, Samuel J. 87
Timezones 89
Tobacco 19, 26, 34
Tocqueville, Alexis de 75
Tombstone, Arizona 94
Torrio, John 125
Toscanini, Arturo 134
Toussaint L'Ouverture, François-Dominique 46
Townsend Acts of 1767 34–35
Toynbee, Arnold 151
Trail of Tears 60, 61
Travis, William Barret 65
Trenton, New Jersey 37
Troup, Robert William, Jr. 115
Troy, New York 96
Truman, Harry 148, 152, 155, 172
Truth, Sojourner 84, 85
Tubac River, Arizona 20, 21
Tubman, Harriet 76, 77
Turkey: World War I 118
Twain, Mark 57, 72, 79

U

Underground Railroad 76, 77
Union Pacific Railroad 88
United Artists 126
United Nations Security Council 155, 174, 183
United States: Bicentennial 151; foreign perceptions 75, 151, 181; nighttime photo 150–51; *see also individual historical events*
U.S. Capitol, Washington, D.C. 140, 141
U.S. Constitution 6, 29, 30, 40; Bill of Rights 6, 21, 40; 13th Amendment 84, 87; 14th Amendment 84, 87, 156; 15th Amendment 84, 87; 18th Amendment 125; 19th Amendment 123; 21st Amendment 125
U.S. Department of the Interior 11
U.S. Postal Service 79
U.S. Steel Corporation 96–97, 137; map 97
U.S. Supreme Court: *Brown v. Board of Education* 156, 157; *Dred Scott v. Sandford* 80; *Plessy v. Ferguson* 156, 157; *Shelly v. Kraemer* 157; *Smith v. Allwright* 156; *United States v. Nixon* 171
Utah 122, 132

V

Vail, Alfred 104
Valentino, Rudolph 126
Valley Forge, Pennsylvania 36, 37
Van Buren, Martin 62
Vanderbilt, Cornelius 97
Van Doren, Charles 152
Vermont 45
Verranzo, Giovanni da 18
Versailles, Treaty of (1919) 121
Vespucci, Amerigo 16
Vietnam War (1959-1975) 153, 162–64, 165
Vikings 9, 12, 13
Vinland, North America 12
Virginia: American Revolution 37; colonial period 18–19, 31; readmission to Union 87; slavery 24, 26; western boundary 45
Virginia Company 19
Voss, James S. 187
Voting Rights Act of 1965 159

W

Wabash and Erie Canal 52
Waco, Texas 180
Walker, Joseph 56
Wallace, Lew 94
Warsaw Pact 172

Washington, D.C.: civil rights marches 157, 159; John F. Kennedy's funeral 160; plan 41; Vietnam War protests 162, 163, 165
Washington, George 28–29, 35, 36, 37, 40
Washington-on-Brazos, Texas 62
Watergate scandal 170–71
Watts riot 157
Weehawken, New Jersey 40
Weld, Theodore Dwight and Angelina 84
Welles, Orson 134–35
Wells, Henry 73
West (region): cowboys 92, 93; land sales 68–69, 71; outlaws 93–94; railroads 88
Westborough, Massachusetts 42
Western Hemisphere: early map 8–9
Western Union 104
Westward expansion 45, 56, 57, 70–71, 100
Wethersfield, Connecticut 30
White, Ed 167
Whitefield, George 21
Whitman, Marcus 56
Whitman, Walt 9
Whitney, Courtney 154, 155
Whitney, Eli 6, 42–43, 55
Whitney, Richard 137
Wilhelm, Kaiser (Germany) 121
William III, King (England) 21
Williams, Arizona 115
Williams, Roger 21
Wilson, Edith 121
Wilson, Woodrow 11, 107, 118, 121, 122
Windsor, Connecticut 30
Wister, Owen 93
Woman's Christian Temperance Union (WCTU) 124
Women: labor 99, 122, 145; voting rights 122–23; World War II 145
Woods, Rose Mary 171
Woodward, Bob 171
Works Progress Administration (WPA) 138, 139
World Trade Center, New York, New York 180, 181
World War I 107, 118–21, 122, 156
World War II 116, 144–48; D-Day 106–7; Manhattan Project 148; radio broadcasts 135
World Wide Web 178
Wounded Knee, Battle of 141, 142–43
Wright brothers 108, 109
Wyeth, N. C. 17
Wyoming 122

Y

Yeager, Chuck 166, 167
Yellowstone National Park 100, 101
Yippies 165
Yorktown, Virginia 37
Yosemite Valley, California 100, 101
Yucatán Peninsula, Mexico 16

Z

Zhou Enlai 173

ILLUSTRATIONS

2-3, LOC, LC-USZC4-8174; 4, Brooklyn Museum/CORBIS; 7, LOC, LC-USZC4-7934; 8-9, Mike Agliolo/CORBIS; 11, William Albert Allard, National Geographic Photographer; 13, Bibliotheque Nationale de France; 14-15, Raymond Gehman/NG Image Collection; 16, Stapleton Collection/CORBIS; 17, N.C. Wyeth/LOC, LC-USZC2-3751; 19, Richard Nowitz/NG Image Collection; 20, The British Library; 22-23, Gunter Marx Photography/CORBIS; 25, LOC, LC-USZ62-44000; 26-27, Andrew J. Russell/LOC, LC-USZ62-27657; 28-29, LOC, LC-USZC4-737; 31, LOC, G3300 1755.M51 vault; 32-33, Ira Block/NG Image Collection; 35, LOC, FP-XVIII-R452; 36, Percy Moran/LOC, LC-USZ62-51810; 38, LOC, LC-USZ62-96219; 39, LOC, LC-USZ62-5781; 41, LOC; 43, F.L. Howe/LOC, LC-USZ62-89498; 44-45, LOC, LC-USZCN4-375; 47, LOC, LC-USZC4-12953; 48, The Academy of Natural Sciences of Philadelphia, Ewell Sale Stewart Library; 49, LOC, G.4126,S12 1806 L4 VAULT; 50, American Philosophical Society; 52, The Historic New Orleans Collection; 53, LOC, LC-USZC4-45990; 54, Lewis Hine/LOC, LC-DIG-nclc-05462; 57, Association of American Railroads; 58-59, Michael Lewis/NG Image Collection; 61, Woolaroc Museum, Bartlesville Oklahoma; 63, LOC, LC-USZ62-110029; 64, Vince Streano/CORBIS; 66-67, Hulton Archive/Getty Images; 69, Western History Collections, University of Oklahoma Libraries; 70, LOC, LC-USZC4-668; 72, LOC, LC-USZ62-120295; 73, Courtesy of the California History Room, California State Library, Sacramento, CA; 74-75, LOC, LC-DIG-cwpb-02731; 77, Hulton Archive/Getty Images; 78, Bettmann/CORBIS; 80, LOC, LC-USZC4-4579; 81, LOC, LC-B8171-7949; 82, LOC, LC-B811-334A; 85, LOC, LC-USZC4-6165; 86, Collection of The New-York Historical Society, Neg. #50470; 89, Alfred A. Hart/LOC, LC-USZ62-56988; 90-91, Special Collections Division, University of Washington Libraries; 92, Christie's Images/CORBIS; 95, Denver Public Library, Western History Collection; 96, LOC, LC-USZ62-61409; 97, Geography & Map Division, LOC; 98, Brown Brothers; 101, Underwood & Underwood/LOC, LCUSZC4-4698; 102-103, Michael Nichols, NGP; 104, LOC, LC-USZ62-75483; 105, LOC, LC-G9-Z2-28608-B; 106-107, Robert F. Sargent/LOC, LC-USZC4-4731; 109, LOC, LC-

W86-35; 110-111, Clyde H. Sunderland/LOC, LC-USZ62-111417; 112, LOC, LC-B2-132-11; 113, LOC, LC-DIG-nclc-01137; 114, Hulton Archives/Getty Images; 116-117, LOC, LC-USF34-005008-D; 118, Howard Chandler Christy/LOC, LC-USZC4-2011; 119, LOC, LC-USZ62-73763; 120-121, National Archives and Records Administration; 122, LOC, LC-B2-2461-14; 123, LOC, LC-USZ62-78691; 124, LOC, LC-USZ62-123257; 126, LOC, LC-B2-6486-3; 127, Hulton Archive/Getty Images; 128-129, Bettmann/CORBIS; 130, LOC, LC-USZ62-95433; 131, LOC, LC-USZC4-4656; 132, LOC, LC-USZ62-29125; 134, Harry S. Mueller/LOC, LC-USZC4-7575; 135, LOC, LC-USZ62-118977; 136, LOC, LC-USZ62-91536; 138, LOC, LC-USZC2-1012; 139, LOC, LC-USF33-000067-M3; 140, LOC, LC-F8-22168; 142-143, James A. Miller/LOC, LC-USZ62-133722; 144, LOC, LC-USZC4-5602; 145, Courtesy Naval Historical Foundation; 147, LOC, LC-USZ62-107559; 149, LOC, LC-USZ62-39852; 150-151, NASA; 152, Hulton Archive/Getty Images; 153, Hulton Archive/Getty Images; 154, LOC, LC-USZ62-70920; 157, LOC, LC-USZ62-35347; 158-159, Jack Delano/LOC, LC-USF33-020522-M2; 160, Marion S. Trikosko/LOC, LC-DIG-ppmsc-01274; 161, Time & Life Pictures/Getty Images; 162, Wally McNamee/CORBIS; 163, Patrick Christian/Getty Images; 164, Bettmann/CORBIS; 166, NASA; 167, NASA; 168-169, Neil A. Armstrong/NASA; 170, Bettmann/CORBIS; 172, LOC, LC-USZCN4-290; 173, Staff SGT. F. Lee Cochran/Department of Defense; 175, Steve McCurry; 176-177, SrA Gudrun Cook/Department of Defense; 178, CERN; 180, Rex A. Stucky/NG Image Collection; 181, Ira Block/NG Image Collection; 182, Staff Sgt. Stacy L. Pearsall/Department of Defense; 184-185, Tech. Sgt. Maria J. Bare/Department of Defense; 186, Charles Nicklin; 187, James S. Voss/NASA; cover, CORBIS; backcover (UP LE), LOC, LC-DIG-nclc-05462; (UP RT), LOC, LC-USZ62-111417; (LO LE), NASA; (LO RT), Department of Defense

UNITED STATES

AN ILLUSTRATED HISTORY
by Ron Fisher

Published by the National Geographic Society

John M. Fahey, Jr., President and Chief Executive Officer

Gilbert M. Grosvenor, Chairman of the Board

Nina D. Hoffman, Executive Vice President;
  President, Book Publishing Group

Prepared by the Book Division

Kevin Mulroy, Senior Vice President and Publisher

Leah Bendavid-Val, Director of Photography Publishing
  and Illustrations

Marianne R. Koszorus, Director of Design

Barbara Brownell Grogan, Executive Editor

Elizabeth Newhouse, Director of Travel Publishing

Carl Mehler, Director of Maps

Staff for This Book

Amy Briggs, Editor

Dana Chivvis, Illustrations Editor

Melissa Farris, Art Director

Mary Beth Keegan, Copy Editor and Researcher

Michael Horenstein, Production Project Manager

Cameron Zotter, Design Specialist

Marshall Kiker, Illustrations Specialist

Jennifer A. Thornton, Managing Editor

Gary Colbert, Production Director

Manufacturing and Quality Management

Christopher A. Liedel, Chief Financial Officer

Phillip L. Schlosser, Vice President

John T. Dunn, Technical Director

Chris Brown, Director

Maryclare Tracy, Manager

Nicole Elliott, Manager

Founded in 1888, the National Geographic Society is one of the largest nonprofit scientific and educational organizations in the world. It reaches more than 285 million people worldwide each month through its official journal, NATIONAL GEOGRAPHIC, and its four other magazines; the National Geographic Channel; television documentaries; radio programs; films; books; videos and DVDs; maps; and interactive media. National Geographic has funded more than 8,000 scientific research projects and supports an education program combating geographic illiteracy.

For more information, please call
1-800-NGS LINE (647-5463)
or write to the following address:

National Geographic Society
1145 17th Street N.W.
Washington, D.C. 20036-4688 U.S.A.

Visit us online at www.nationalgeographic.com

For information about special discounts for bulk purchases, please contact National Geographic Books Special Sales: ngspecsales@ngs.org

For rights or permissions inquiries, please contact National Geographic Books Subsidiary Rights: ngbookrights@ngs.org

Library of Congress Cataloging-in-Publication Data

Fisher, Ron, 1938-
   The United States : an illustrated history / text adapted by Ron Fisher.
      p. cm.
   Includes index.
   ISBN-13: 978-1-4262-0200-1 (regular)
   ISBN-13: 978-1-4262-0201-8 (deluxe)
   1. United States--History--Pictorial works. 2. United States--History. 3. United States--History--Pictorial works. I. Title.
   E178.5.F57 2007
   973--dc22
                                    2007023414

ISBN-13: 978-1-4262-0200-1
ISBN-13 (Deluxe): 978-1-4262-0201-8
Printed in U.S.A.